Climbing a Few of Japan's 100 Famous Mountains –

Volume 10:
Mt. Mizugaki

Daniel H. Wieczorek and Kazuya Numazawa

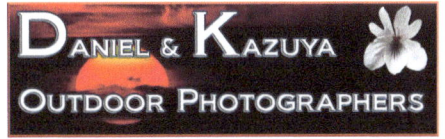

Climbing a Few of Japan's 100 Famous Mountains –

Volume 10:
Mt. Mizugaki

ISBN-10: 1500235288
ISBN-13: 978-1500235284

Rev. 2

DEDICATION

This work is dedicated, first of all, to my partner, Kazuya Numazawa. He always keeps my interest in photography up and makes me keep striving for the perfect photo. He also often makes me think of the expression "when the going gets tough, the tough keep going." Without my partner it has to also be noted that I most likely would not have climbed any of these mountains.

Secondly, it is dedicated to my mother and father, bless them, for tolerating and even encouraging my photography hobby from the time I was 12 years old.

And, finally, it is dedicated to my friends who have encouraged me to create books of photographs which I have taken while doing mountain climbing.

Some other books by Daniel H. Wieczorek and Kazuya Numazawa

"Outdoor Photography of Japan: Through the Seasons"; ISBN/EAN13: 146110520X / 9781461105206; 362 Pages; June 10, 2011; Also available as a Kindle Edition

"Some Violets of Eastern Japan – 2ⁿᵈ Edition"; ISBN/EAN13: 1499262809 / 9781499262803; 118 Pages; April 26, 2014; Also available as a Kindle Edition

"A Pocket-Size Version of Some Violets of Eastern Japan – 2ⁿᵈ Edition"; ISBN/EAN13: 1499261446 / 9781499261448; 122 Pages; April 26, 2014

"Climbing a Few of Japan's 100 Famous Mountains – Volume 1: Mt. Daisetsu (Mt. Asahidake)"; ISBN/EAN13: 1493777203 / 9781493777204; 66 Pages; December 5, 2013; Also available as a Kindle Edition

"Climbing a Few of Japan's 100 Famous Mountains – Volume 2: Mt. Chokai (Choukai)"; ISBN/EAN13: 1494368404 / 9781494368401; 72 Pages; December 8, 2013; Also available as a Kindle Edition

"Climbing a Few of Japan's 100 Famous Mountains – Volume 3: Mt. Gassan"; ISBN/EAN13: 149487217X / 9781494872175; 70 Pages; January 4, 2014; Also available as a Kindle Edition

"Climbing a Few of Japan's 100 Famous Mountains – Volume 4: Mt. Hakkoda & Mt. Zao"; ISBN/EAN13: 1495396568 / 9781495396564; 88 Pages; January 31, 2014; Also available as a Kindle Edition

"Climbing a Few of Japan's 100 Famous Mountains – Volume 5: Mt. Kumotori"; ISBN/EAN13: 1495980529 / 9781495980527; 84 Pages; February 17, 2014; Also available as a Kindle Edition

"A Pocket-Size Version of Climbing a Few of Japan's 100 Famous Mountains – Volume 5: Mt. Kumotori"; ISBN/EAN13: 1497444942 / 9781497444942; 90 Pages; March 25, 2014

"Climbing a Few of Japan's 100 Famous Mountains – Volume 6: Mt. Shirane (Kusatsu)"; ISBN/EAN13: 1497303230 / 9781497303232; 80 Pages; March 11, 2014; Also available as a Kindle Edition

"Climbing a Few of Japan's 100 Famous Mountains – Volume 7: Mt. Shibutsu"; ISBN/EAN13: 1497539277 / 9781497539273; 80 Pages; April 4, 2014; Also available as a Kindle Edition

"Climbing a Few of Japan's 100 Famous Mountains – Volume 8: Mt. Kiso-Komagatake"; ISBN/EAN13: 1499178638 / 9781499178630; 72 Pages; April 18, 2014; Also available as a Kindle Edition

"Climbing a Few of Japan's 100 Famous Mountains – Volume 9: Mt. Kitadake"; ISBN/EAN13: 1499786085 / 9781499786088; 62 Pages; June 4, 2014; Also available as a Kindle Edition

FOREWORD

What is the purpose of this series of books? It is to show you, in photographs, some of the astounding sights and scenery we have seen while climbing the mountains included herein. At this time we have climbed 14 of Japan's 100 Famous Mountains. The ones we have climbed are: 1) Mt. Daisetsu (2,290 m) (大雪山) = Mt. Asahidake (旭岳); 2) Mt. Chokai (2,236 m) (鳥海山); 3) Mt. Gassan (1,984 m) (月山); 4) Mt. Hakkoda (1,584 m) (八甲田山); 5) Mt. Zao (1,841 m) (蔵王山); 6) Mt. Kumotori (2,017 m) (雲取山); 7) Mt. Kusatsu-Shirane (2,171 m) (草津白根山); 8) Mt. Shibutsu (2,228 m) (至仏山); 9) Mt. Kiso-Komagatake (2,956 m) (木曾駒ヶ岳); 10) Mt. Kitadake (North Peak) (3,192 m) (北岳); 11) Mt. Mizugaki (2,230 m) (瑞牆山); 12) Mt. Shiroumadake (2,932 m) (白馬岳); 13) Mt. Tateyama (3,015 m) (立山); and 14) Mt. Yatsugatake (2,899 m) (八ヶ岳).

By the way, I (Daniel) did all of the writing and Kazuya did a fair percentage of the photography. So, do not be surprised from time to time when you see references such as "Kazuya" and "that's me…".

Daniel and Kazuya's *"Outdoor Photography of Japan: Through the Seasons"* includes some of the same photos as this work, but this work may be thought of as a subset of that work because that work includes adventures to many mountains beyond the 14 famous mountains which are found in this series of books. In addition, the photos in that book were more than 50% flower photos. This series includes less than 1% flower photos, and only where the flower is a part of a mountain scene. In addition, this series includes many photos which were not included in that work.

TABLE OF CONTENTS

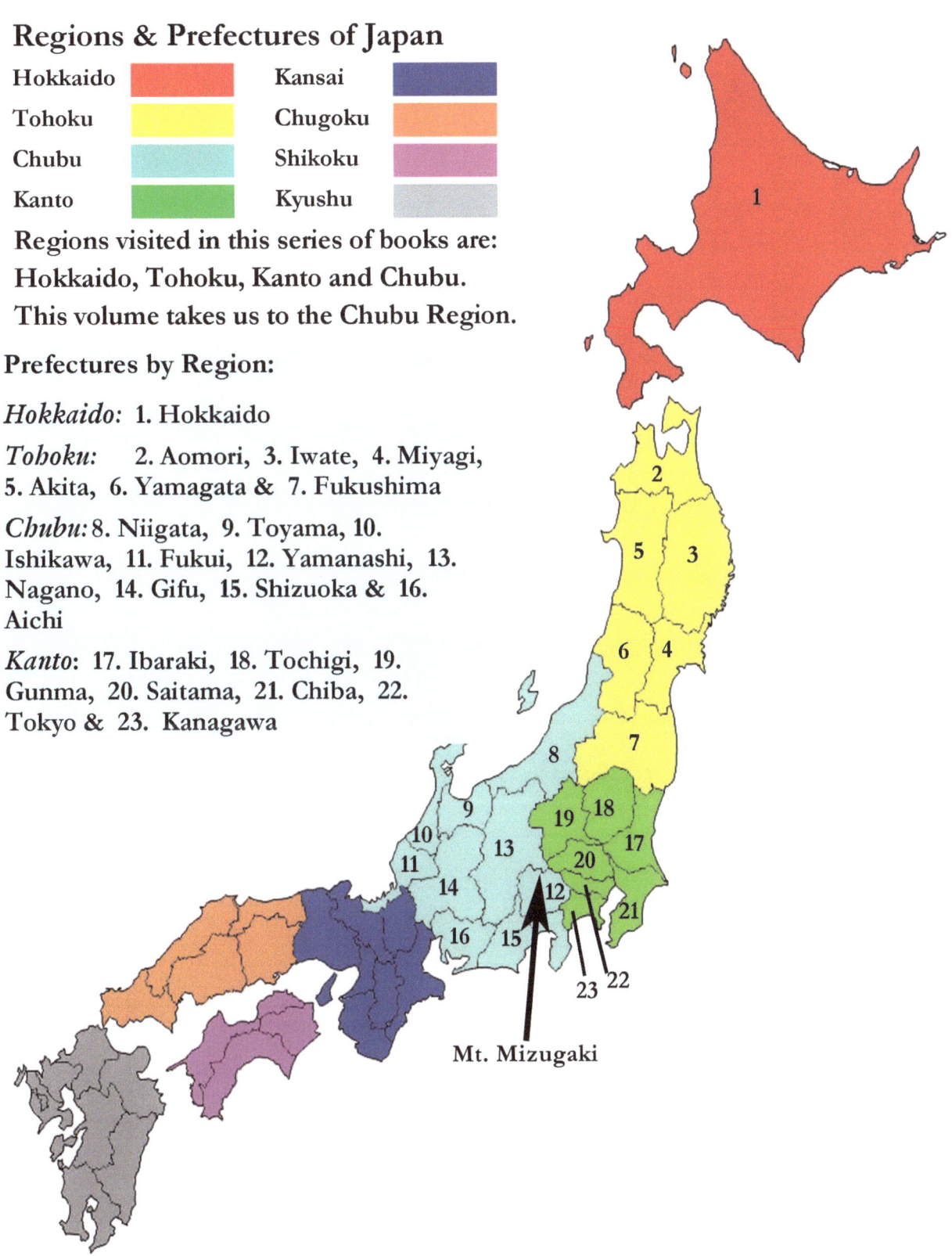

Regions & Prefectures of Japan

Hokkaido

Tohoku

Chubu

Kanto

Kansai

Chugoku

Shikoku

Kyushu

Regions visited in this series of books are: Hokkaido, Tohoku, Kanto and Chubu. This volume takes us to the Chubu Region.

Prefectures by Region:

Hokkaido: 1. Hokkaido

Tohoku: 2. Aomori, 3. Iwate, 4. Miyagi, 5. Akita, 6. Yamagata & 7. Fukushima

Chubu: 8. Niigata, 9. Toyama, 10. Ishikawa, 11. Fukui, 12. Yamanashi, 13. Nagano, 14. Gifu, 15. Shizuoka & 16. Aichi

Kanto: 17. Ibaraki, 18. Tochigi, 19. Gunma, 20. Saitama, 21. Chiba, 22. Tokyo & 23. Kanagawa

Mt. Mizugaki

1) JAPAN'S 100 FAMOUS MOUNTAINS

What are Japan's 100 famous mountains? A selection of famous mountains in Japan has been compiled since the Edo period (1603 – 1867) and the list has been revised several times since the very first list appeared. At the current time the list of 100 famous mountains includes those shown below. Also shown is the Japanese pronunciation, elevation in meters and feet, the Japanese kanji, the Region the mountain is in and a few a.k.a. (also known as) names.

Hokkaido:

1.	Mt. Akan (Akandake)	1,499	4,918	阿寒岳
2.	**Mt. Asahi (Asahidake) a.k.a.**			
	Mt. Daisetsu (Daisetsuzan)	**2,290**	**7,513**	**旭岳 a.k.a. (大雪山)**
3.	Mt. Poroshiri (Poroshiridake)	2,052	6,734	幌尻岳
4.	Mt. Rausu (Rausudake)	1,660	5,446	羅臼岳
5.	Mt. Rishiri (Rishiridake)	1,721	5,646	利尻岳
6.	Mt. Shari (Sharidake)	1,545	5,069	斜里岳
7.	Mt. Tokachi (Tochidake)	2,077	6,814	十勝岳
8.	Mt. Tomuraushi (Tomuraushiyama)	2,141	7,024	トムラウシ山
9.	Mt. Yotei (Yoteizan) a.k.a.			
	(Mt. Shiribeshi) (Shiribeshiyama)	1,893	6,211	羊蹄山 a.k.a. (後方羊蹄山)

Tohoku Region:

10.	Mt. Adatara (Adatarayama)	1,700	5,577	安達太良山
11.	Mt. Aizu-Komagatake (Aizukomagatake)	2,132	6,995	会津駒ケ岳
12.	Mt. Asahi (Asahirenpou)	1,870	6,135	朝日連峰
13.	Mt. Azuma (Azumayama)	2,035	6,676	吾妻山
14.	Mt. Bandai (Bandaisan)	1,819	5,968	磐梯山
15.	**Mt. Chōkai (Chōkaisan)**	**2,236**	**7,336**	**鳥海山**
16.	**Mt. Gassan (Gassan)**	**1,984**	**6,509**	**月山**
17.	Mt. Hachimantai (Hachimantai)	1,614	5,295	八幡平
18.	**Mt. Hakkōda (Hakkōdasan)**	**1,584**	**5,197**	**八甲田山**
19.	Mt. Hayachine (Hayachinesan)	1,917	6,289	早池峰山
20.	Mt. Hiuchigatake (Hiuchigatake)	2,356	7,730	燧ケ岳
21.	Mt. Iide (Iiderenpou)	2,105	6,906	飯豊連峰
22.	Mt. Iwaki (Iwakisan)	1,625	5,331	岩木山
23.	Mt. Iwate (Iwatesan)	2,038	6,686	岩手山
24.	**Mt. Zaō (Zaōsan)**	**1,841**	**6,040**	**蔵王山**

Kanto Region:

25.	Mt. Akagi (Akagiyama)	1,828	5,997	赤城山
26.	Mt. Asama (Asamayama)	2,568	8,425	浅間山

No.	Name	Meters	Feet	Kanji
27.	Mt. Azumaya (Azumayasan)	2,354	7,723	四阿山
28.	Mt. Hiragatake (Hiragatake)	2,141	7,024	平ヶ岳
29.	Mt. Hotaka (Hotakayama)	2,158	7,080	武尊山
30.	**Mt. Kumotori (Kumotoriyama)**	**2,017**	**6,617**	**雲取山**
31.	**Mt. Kusatsu-Shirane (Kusatsu-Shiranesan)**	**2,171**	**7,123**	**草津白根山**
32.	Mt. Nantai (Nantaisan)	2,486	8,156	男体山
33.	Mt. Nasu (Nasudake)	1,915	6,283	那須岳
34.	Mt. Nikko-Shirane (Nikko-Shiranesan)	2,578	8,458	日光白根山
35.	Mt. Ryokami (Ryoukamisan)	1,723	5,653	両神山
36.	**Mt. Shibutsu (Shibutsusan)**	**2,228**	**7,310**	**至仏山**
37.	Mt. Sukai (Sukaisan)	2,144	7,034	皇海山
38.	Mt. Tanigawa (Tanigawadake)	1,963	6,440	谷川岳
39.	Mt. Tanzawa (Tanzawasan)	1,567	5,141	丹沢山
40.	Mt. Tsukuba (Tsukubasan)	877	2,877	筑波山

Chubu Region:

No.	Name	Meters	Feet	Kanji
41.	Mt. Ainodake (Ainodake)	3,189	10,463	間ノ岳
42.	Mt. Akaishi (Akaishidake)	3,120	10,236	赤石岳
43.	Mt. Amagi (Amagisan)	1,406	4,613	天城山
44.	Mt. Amakazari (Amakazariyama)	1,963	6,440	雨飾山
45.	Mt. Daibosatsu (Daibosatsurei)	2,057	6,749	大菩薩嶺
46.	Mt. Ena (Enasan)	2,191	7,188	恵那山
47.	Mt. Fuji (Fujisan)	3,776	12,388	富士山
48.	Mt. Goryū (Goryūdake)	2,814	9,232	五竜岳
49.	Mt. Hakusan (Hakusan)	2,702	8,865	白山
50.	Mt. Hijiri (Hijiridake)	3,013	9,885	聖岳
51.	Mt. Hiuchi (Hiuchiyama)	2,462	8,077	火打山
52.	Mt. Hōō (Hōōsan)	2,840	9,318	鳳凰山
53.	Mt. Hotaka (Hotakadake)	3,190	10,466	穂高岳
54.	Mt. Jōnen (Jōnendake)	2,857	9,373	常念岳
55.	Mt. Kai-Komagatake (Kaikomagatake)	2,967	9,734	甲斐駒ケ岳
56.	Mt. Kasa (Kasagatake)	2,897	9,505	笠ヶ岳
57.	Mt. Kashima Yarigatake (Kashimayarigatake)	2,889	9,478	鹿島槍ヶ岳
58.	Mt. Kinpu (Kinpusan)	2,599	8,527	金峰山
59.	Mt. Kirigamine (Kirigamine)	1,925	6,316	霧ヶ峰
60.	**Mt. Kiso-Komagatake (Kisokomagatake)**	**2,956**	**9,698**	**木曽駒ケ岳**
61.	**Mt. Kitadake (Kitadake)**	**3,192**	**10,472**	**北岳**
62.	Mt. Kobushi (Kobushidake)	2,475	8,120	甲武信岳

63.	Mt. Kuro (Kurodake) a.k.a.			
	(Mt. Suisho) (Suishodake)	2,978	9,770	黒岳 a.k.a. (水晶岳)
64.	Mt. Kurobe-Gorō (Kurobegorōdake)	2,840	9,318	黒部五郎岳
65.	Mt. Makihata (Makihatayama)	1,967	6,453	巻機山
66.	**Mt. Mizugaki (Mizugakiyama)**	**2,230**	**7,316**	**瑞牆山**
67.	Mt. Myoko (Myokosan)	2,454	8,051	妙高山
68.	Mt. Naeba (Naebasan)	2,145	7,037	苗場山
69.	Mt. Norikura (Norikuradake)	3,026	9,928	乗鞍岳
70.	Mt. Ontake (Ontakesan)	3,067	10,062	御嶽山
71.	Mt. Senjōgatake (Senjōgatake)	3,033	9,951	仙丈ケ岳
72.	Mt. Shiomi (Shiomidake)	3,047	9,997	塩見岳
73.	**Mt. Shiroumadake (Shiroumadake)**	**2,932**	**9,619**	**白馬岳**
74.	Mt. Takatsuma (Takatsumayama)	2,353	7,720	高妻山
75.	Mt. Tateshina (Tateshinayama)	2,530	8,301	蓼科山
76.	**Mt. Tateyama (Tateyama)**	**3,015**	**9,892**	**立山**
77.	Mt. Tekari (Tekaridake)	2,591	8,501	光岳
78.	Mt. Tsurugi (Tsurugidake)	2,999	9,839	劔岳
79.	Mt. Uonuma-Komagatake a.k.a.			
	(Echigo-Komagatake) 2,003	6,572		魚沼駒ヶ岳 a.k.a. (越後駒ケ岳)
80.	Mt. Utsugi (Utsugidake)	2,864	9,396	空木岳
81.	Mt. Warusawa (Warusawadake)	3,141	10,305	悪沢岳
82.	Mt. Washiba (Washibadake)	2,924	9,593	鷲羽岳
83.	Mt. Yake (Yakedake)	2,444	8,018	焼岳
84.	Mt. Yakushi (Yakushidake)	2,926	9,600	薬師岳
85.	Mt. Yarigatake (Yarigatake)	3,180	10,433	槍ヶ岳
86.	**Mt. Yatsugatake (Yatsugatake)**	**2,899**	**9,511**	**八ヶ岳**
87.	Utsukushigahara Highland			
	(Utsukushigahara)	2,034	6,673	美ヶ原

Western Japan:

88.	Mt. Arashima (Arashimadake)	1,523	4,997	荒島岳
89.	Mt. Aso (Asosan)	1,592	5,223	阿蘇山
90.	Mt. Daisen (Daisen)	1,729	5,673	大山
91.	Mt. Ibuki (Ibukiyama)	1,377	4,518	伊吹山
92.	Mt. Ishizuchi (Ishizuchisan)	1,982	6,503	石鎚山
93.	Mt. Kaimon (Kaimondake)	924	3,031	開聞岳
94.	Mt. Kirishima (Kirishimayama)	1,700	5,577	霧島山
95.	Mt. Kujū (Kujūsan)	1,791	5,876	九重山
96.	Mt. Miya-no-ura (Miyanouradake)	1,936	6,352	宮之浦岳
97.	Mt. Ōmine (Ōminesan)	1,915	6,283	大峰山
98.	Mt. Sobo (Sobosan)	1,756	5,761	祖母山

99. Mt. Tsurugi (Tsurugisan)	1,955	6,414	剣山
100. The Wide Mountain of Ōdai (Ōdaigaharayama)	1,695	5,561	大台ケ原山

My partner and I have climbed (or in one, case merely ascended) the 14 mountains which are **shaded, underlined and in bold** text. You'll probably note that we have not climbed Mt. Fuji and wonder why? The reason is simple – too many people and not enough interesting sights.

Using photographs and a minimum amount of text we are telling (showing) you the stories of climbing the 14 mountains shown above. We started at the beginning of the 100 mountains list and are working our way through it. That means that the first climb we showed you, in Volume 1, was on Hokkaido and it was a climb of Mt. Daisetsu (2,290.9 m = 7,516 ft) (大雪山), which is also known as Mt. Asahidake. Mt. Daisetsu is the name of the entire mountain range, while Mount Asahi (旭岳 Asahidake) is the tallest mountain in that mountain range and also the tallest mountain in Hokkaido Prefecture, Japan. It is part of the Daisetsuzan Volcanic Group and it is located in the northern part of Daisetsuzan National Park.

The second mountain we showed you, in Volume 2, was in the Tohoku Region and the mountain name was Mt. Chokai (or Choukai) (2,236 m = 7,336 ft) (鳥海山). Mt. Chokai is located on the southern border of Akita Prefecture and the northern border of Yamagata Prefecture. It is still an active volcano and it is the second tallest mountain in the Tohoku Region of Japan.

The third mountain (Volume 3) was also in the Tohoku Region and it was Mt. Gassan (1,984 m = 6,509 ft) (月山). Mt. Gassan is the highest peak in the Dewa Sanzan trio of sacred mountains. It lies between Mt. Chokai to the north, and Mt. Asahi to the south, in Yamagata Prefecture. Being a sacred mountain, it is famous for the shrine at the summit and in the summer you can often see large groups of white-clothed pilgrims hiking to or from the summit.

The fourth mountain we showed you, in Volume 4, was also in the Tohoku Region of Japan and the mountain was Mt. Hakkoda (1,584 m = 5,197 ft) (八甲田山). The Hakkoda Mountains are a volcanic mountain range that lie south of Aomori City, in Aomori Prefecture Japan. The peak name is actually Mt. Hakkoda – Odake. Odake is the tallest peak in the Hakkoda Range.

The fifth mountain we showed you, also in Volume 4, was Mt. Zao (1,841 m = 6,040 ft) (蔵王山). It was also in the Tohoku Region and also in Yamagata Prefecture. We did not actually make it to the summit of this mountain. We visited it in the winter and it was very cold and windy. We took an automobile as far as possible and then transferred to a gondola car and went only a little bit beyond the top of the gondola – to about the 1,661 m (= 5,449 ft) level of the mountain. We do, however, have some impressive photos from that trip.

The sixth mountain you saw in this series of books (in Volume 5) was Mt. Kumotori (2,017.7 m = 6,620 ft) (雲取山). Mt. Kumotori is in the Kanto Region and the peak divides the prefectures of Tokyo, Yamanashi and Saitama. Its summit is the highest point in Tokyo. It separates the Okutama Mountains and the Okuchichibu Mountains. No matter which direction you choose to come to this mountain from, the summit is a long hike from the nearest bus stop, road end or train station.

The seventh mountain, in Volume 6, was Mt. Kusatsu-Shirane (2,171 m = 7,123 ft) (草津白根山). This peak is also in the Kanto Region of Japan, in Gunma Prefecture. It is called Mt. Kusatsu-Shirane to differentiate it from Mt. Nikko-Shirane, which is on the opposite side of Gunma Prefecture. There is a beautifully colored volcanic pond here known as Yu-gama. Another volcanic pond close-by is Yumiike and there is a dry crater named Karagama Crater.

The eighth mountain we showed you, in Volume 7, also in the Kanto Region, in Gunma Prefecture, was Mt. Shibutsu (2,228 m = 7,310 ft) (至仏山). It separates Oze Marsh (Oze National Park) from the remainder of Gunma Prefecture. It is an interesting mountain composed primarily of serpentinite. There is also a lesser peak known as Mt. Koshibutsu (2,162 m = 7,093 ft).

The ninth mountain we took you to, in Volume 8, was Mt. Kiso-Komagatake (2,956 m = 9,698 ft) (木曾駒ヶ岳). It can be found in Nagano Prefecture, in the Chubu Region. It is located in Japan's Central Alps Mountain Range and is the highest peak in that range.

Then, in Volume 9 we very briefly took you to the tenth of Japan's 100 famous mountains which we have climbed – Mt. Kitadake (North Peak) (3,193 m = 10,476 ft) (北岳). This is Japan's second highest mountain after Mt. Fuji and is known as "the Leader of the Southern Alps". It is in Yamanashi Prefecture, in the Chubu Region.

Mt. Mizugaki (2,230 m = 7,317 ft) (瑞牆山) is the eleventh mountain that will be addressed, in this volume. It too is in the Chubu Region. It is in Yamanashi Prefecture. It lies across the valley from the Southern Alps, slightly southeast of Yatsugatake and northwest of the Daibosatsu ridgeline. Granite towers, blocks and obelisks protrude from the summit of this mountains. It is truly an amazing sight to see from its lower slopes.

Then we'll continue on to the twelfth mountain and that is also in the Chubu Region. It is Mt. Shiroumadake (2,932 m = 9,620 ft) (白馬岳). It is the tallest peak in the Hakuba section of the Hida Mountains, also known as Japan's Northern Alps Mountain Range. It is in Nagano Prefecture.

After that, for the thirteenth mountain, we'll take you to another Chubu Region mountain – Mt. Tateyama (3,015 m = 9,892 ft) (立山). It can be found in the southeastern portion of Toyama Prefecture and it also is a mountain in the Northern Alps Mountain Range, or Hida Mountains. It is one of the tallest peaks in the Hida Mountains and is the highest peak in Toyama Prefecture.

The fourteenth and final mountain we'll cover in this series of books is also in the Chubu Region – Mt. Yatsugatake (Mt. Akadake – 2,899 m = 9,511 ft) (八ヶ岳). Yatsugatake means "eight peaks" and the highest mountain in this range is Mt. Akadake. Actually there are many more than eight peaks, but in Japanese the kanji character for Hachi (八) sometimes implies "many" or "several".

According to legend, Yatsugatake was once higher than Mount Fuji, but Konohana-Sakuyahime, the goddess of Mount Fuji, tore it down out of jealousy, leaving the collection of peaks we have today. This could possibly be true considering that Yatsugatake is older than Fuji and as Fuji rose in prominence Yatsugatake wore away.

Another version of this legend says that a long time ago, Yatsugatake was an ordinary mountain with only one peak, and it was as high as or higher then Mt. Fuji. Yatsugatake's god and Mt. Fuji's goddess began quarreling over their height. Each of them insisted that he/she was taller. The Amitabha Buddha, who was entrusted to arbitrate the dispute, set a valley between the tops of the two mountains and filled it with water. The water submerged the summit of Mt. Fuji, revealing that Yatsugatake was indeed, taller. Mt. Fuji's goddess, who was unyielding, was very angry so she kept striking Yatsugatake with a long stick until it was divided into several peaks, all lower than Mt. Fuji. That is why Mt. Yatsugatake now has so many peaks. Interesting!

By the way – *dake* or *take* (岳) = peak or high peak. Some authors prefer to leave this term off when referring to a Japanese mountain, for example they will refer to Mt. Kitadake as Mt. Kita and use the argument that it is redundant to use the –dake portion of the name. We prefer to use the dake suffix for completeness. If one is to be absolutely correct it should probably be called Kita Peak, not Mt. Kita.

"Mountains are the cathedrals where I practice my religion."
— Anatoli Boukreev

"Climb the mountains and get their good tidings. Nature's peace will flow into you as sunshine flows into trees. The winds will blow their own freshness into you, and the storms their energy, while cares will drop away from you like the leaves of Autumn."
— John Muir, The Mountains of California

"Chasing angels or fleeing demons, go to the mountains."
— Jeffrey Rasley

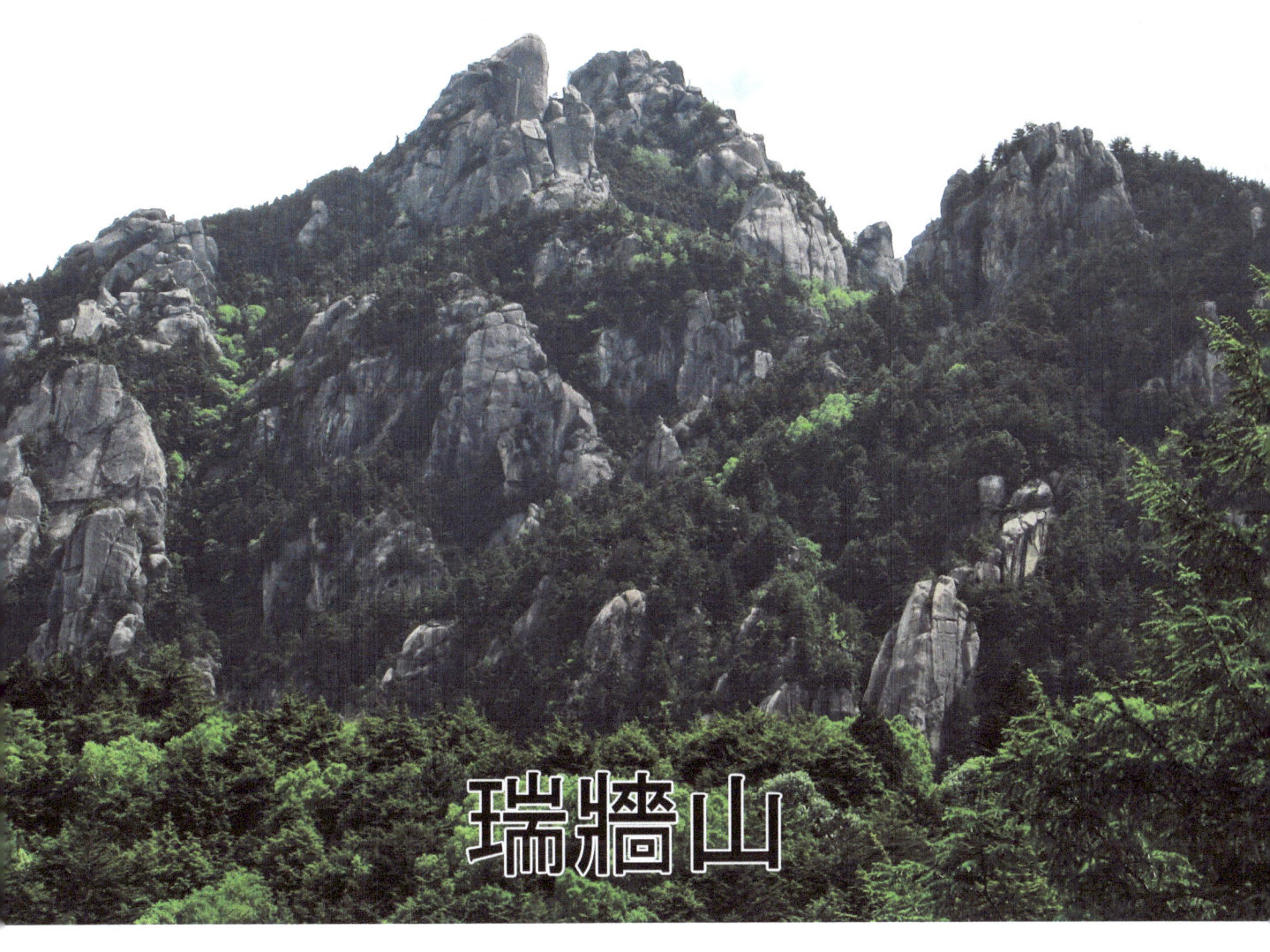

瑞牆山

2) MT. MIZUGAKI

This is the 11th mountain and the 10th climb that we are showing you in this series of books. This – Volume 10 – will take us on a climb in Yamanashi Prefecture, in the Chubu Region of Japan – specifically our single climb of Mt. Mizugaki (2,230.2 m = 7,317 ft) (瑞牆山). Mt. Mizugaki can easily claim that it has the most difficult kanji of all the 100 Famous Mountains of Japan. The kanji is superimposed on the above photo and its meaning is "auspicious wall mountain". By the way, the above photo was taken from a spot about thirty-five minutes into our climb. Most of the signs in the area which direct one to this mountain are written in Hiragana (みずがき) because very few Japanese people can even read the kanji for Mizugaki. The peak area features unique rock formations and superb views of the surrounding mountainous landscape. Mizugaki lies across the valley from the Southern Alps, slightly southeast of Yatsugatake and northwest of the Daibosatsu ridgeline. Granite towers, blocks and obelisks protrude from the summit of this mountain. It is truly an amazing sight to see from its lower, as well as its upper, slopes. This granite mountain's claim to fame is its pillars and cliffs of granodiorite type granite. From the summit of course one can view Mt. Yatsugatake and the Southern Alps Mountain range, plus Mt. Fuji. It is located at the western end of the Oku-Chichibu mountain chain and being composed of large, humped rocks, the mountain has a particular, beautifully strange appearance. It lies very near to Mt. Kinpu (金峰山), the highest peak in the Oku-Chichibu Mountains at 2,598 meters, which is also one of Japan's 100 Famous Mountains.

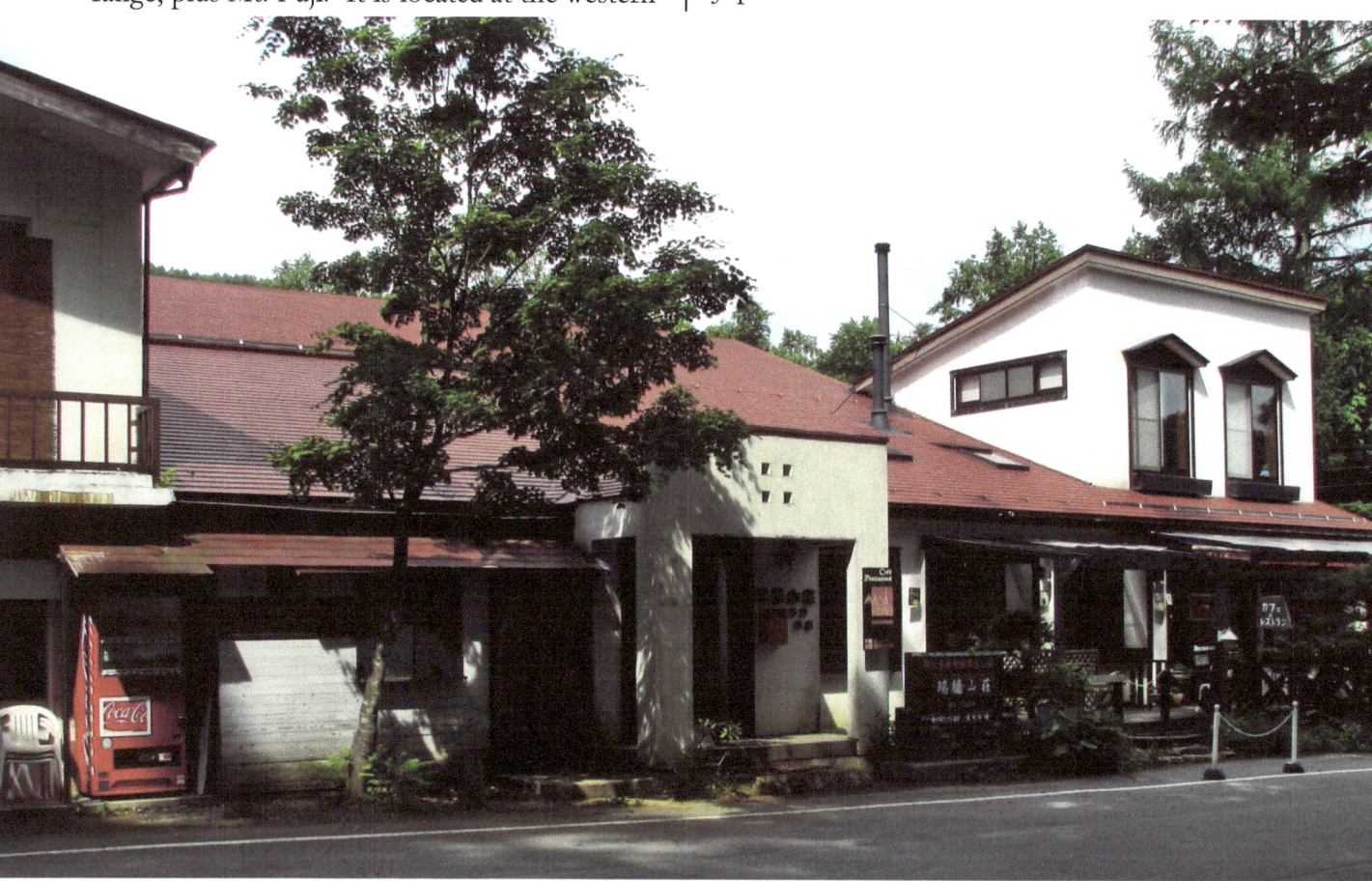

The photo just above shows the starting point for this climb. We arrived at this point via a bus from Nirasaki train station, at about 9:00 AM. This is an inn right here at the bus stop, so if one wants to get a very early start and possibly climb both Mt. Mizugaki and also Mt. Kinpu (金峰山) on the same day, it is most likely possible. We, however, were not in a rush because we like to go slow and enjoy our surroundings. As you probably know if you have read other volumes in this series of books, we also like to search for flowers and spend ample time photographing them. On this particular outing we were in search of a specific species of orchid which we had read was in bloom at a particular place along this trail. We did not find it, but we had a very enjoyable time climbing this mountain. It was not a 100% clear day, but there was plenty of sun and the temperature was nice. We had no complaints.

On the facing page you will find the map which shows how to get to the summit of this mountain. The 1) annotation is at the above inn and bus stop. Also note the 2) and 3) annotations as well as the Summit annotation. We'll talk about these annotations later on.

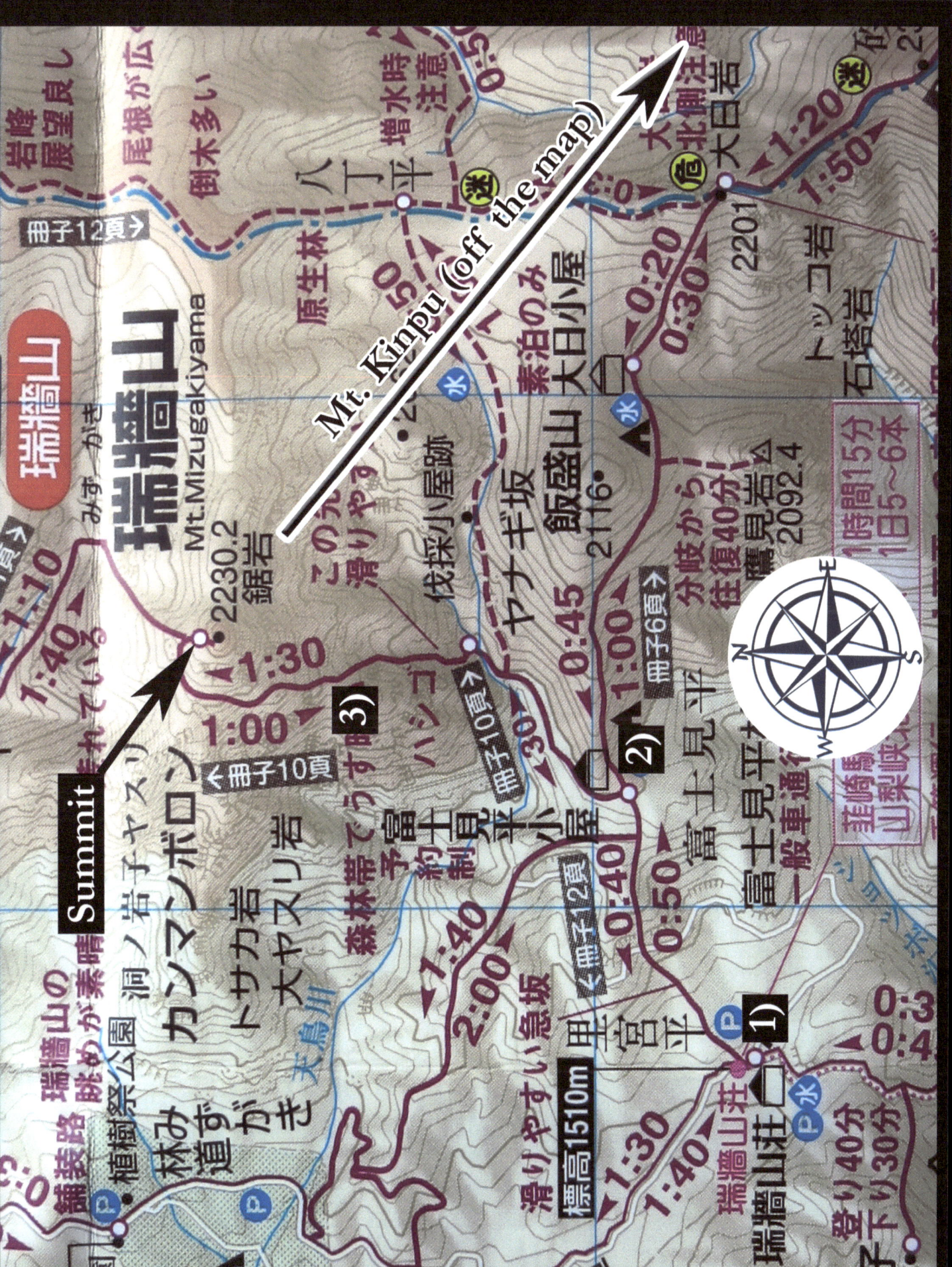

瑞牆山

瑞牆山
Mt.Mizugakiyama

みず がき

瑞牆山

Mt. Kinpu (off the map)

Summit

八丁平

大日平

大日岩

北側注意

2201

トップ岩

右塔岩

増水時注意

倒木多い

原生林！

尾根が広がる

岩峰 展望良し

甲子12頁→

1:10

1:40

すべっている

2230.2
鋸岩

1:30

1:00

←甲子10頁

カンマンボロン

洞ノ岩子岩スベリ

トサカ岩
大ヤスリ岩

森林帯 てらす川

天鳥川

林み道ずがすい

植樹祭公園

瑞牆山の
眺めが素晴

舗装路

P

P

この元
滑り岩やす

伐採小屋跡

ハシゴ

甲子10頁→

0:30

2:40

富士見平小屋

予約制

富士見平

甲子12頁→

濡りやすい急坂

標高1510m

2:00

1:40

1:30

1:40

瑞牆山荘

瑞牆山荘

P

P水

登り40分
下り30分

ヤナギ坂

飯盛山
2116

0:45

0:40

1:00

甲子6頁→

2)

富士見平平

0:50

富士見平
車通行

一般車通行

P

1)

素泊のみ
大日小屋

水

0:20

0:30

0:50

分岐から
往復40分

鷹見岩
2092.4

1:00

鷹見岩

1時間15分
1日5〜6本

韮崎駅
山梨峡

0:3
0:4

N E S W

1:20

1:50

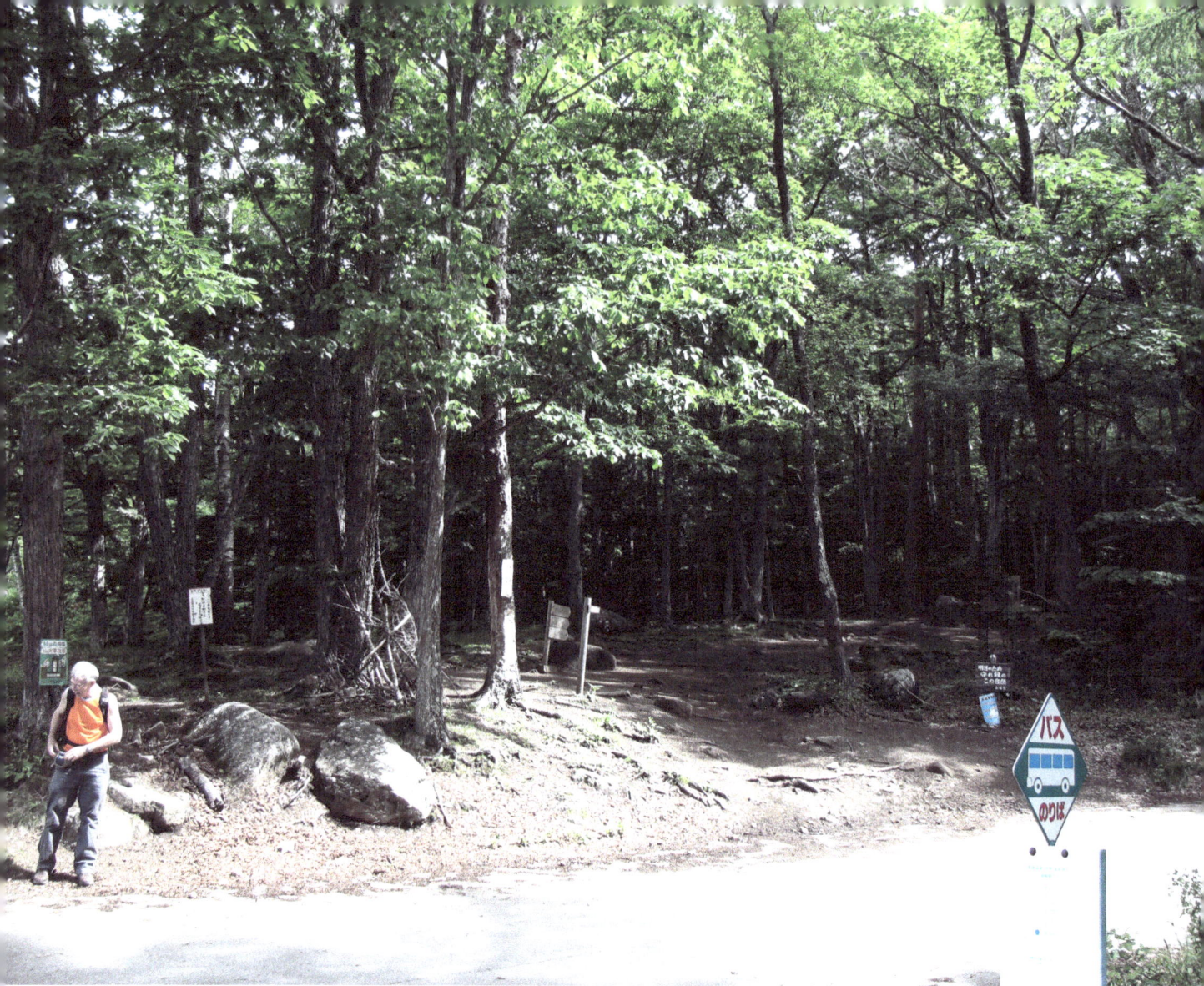

The photo just above was taken from directly in front of the inn shown in the previous photo. That's me on the left edge of the photo. The sign which has the katakana characters バス on it is the bus stop. The trail begins right there across the road from this photo. This photo was taken at 9:08 AM, just as we began our climb. We often try and take some photos right at the start of our climbs so that the camera will record the time for us and we don't have to write it down in some kind of a notebook until later on.

The facing page photo shows one of the few species of flowers which we photographed on this adventure. This is a primrose – specifically *Primula japonica*. It was taken at 9:18 AM, only about ten minutes into the climb and we have already found an interesting and beautiful flower. This species seemed to only grow at the lower elevations, however, as we never saw any of them after we started climbing up to higher elevations. It was dark enough here in the forest so that a flash was necessary to capture this species.

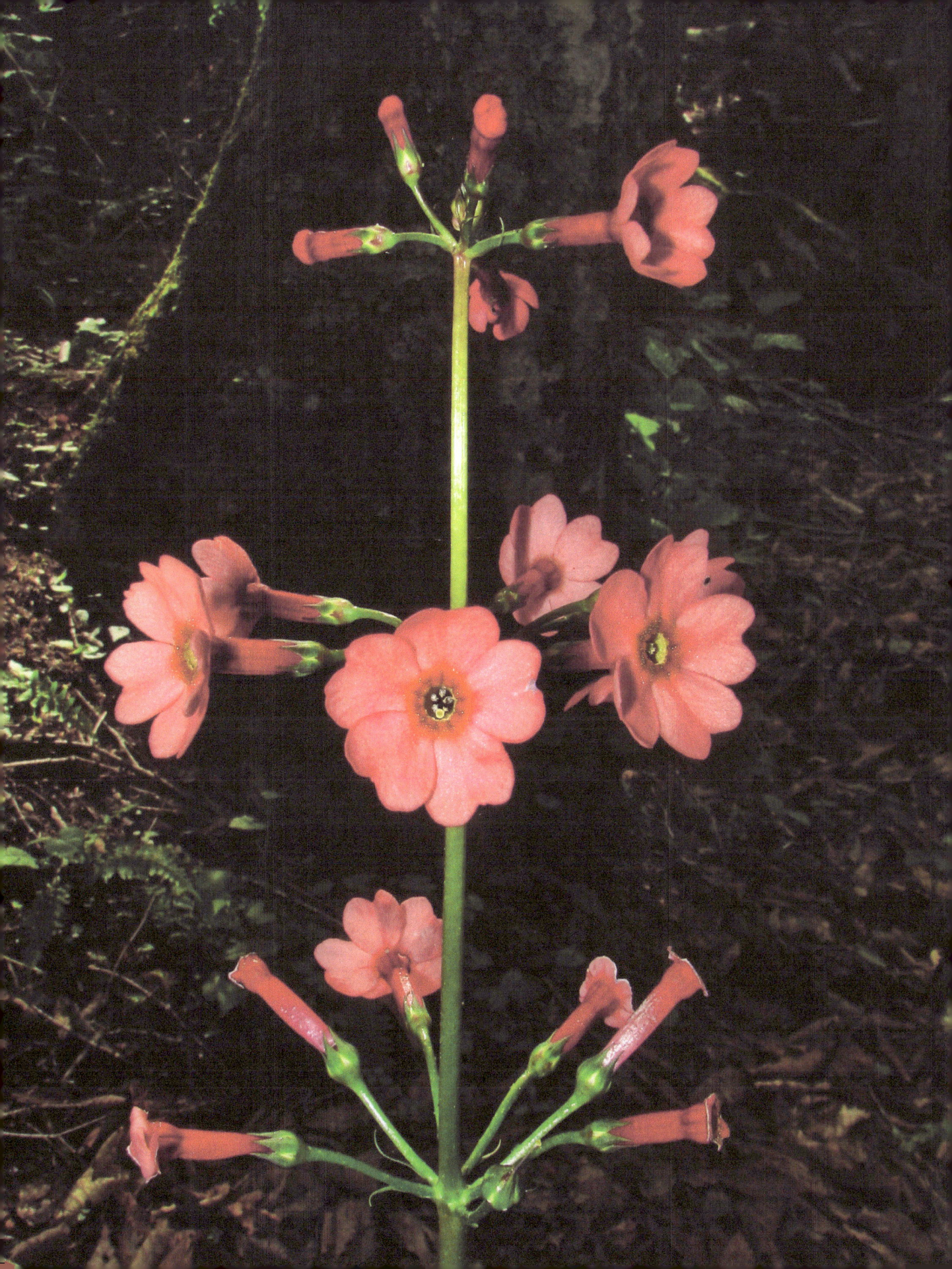

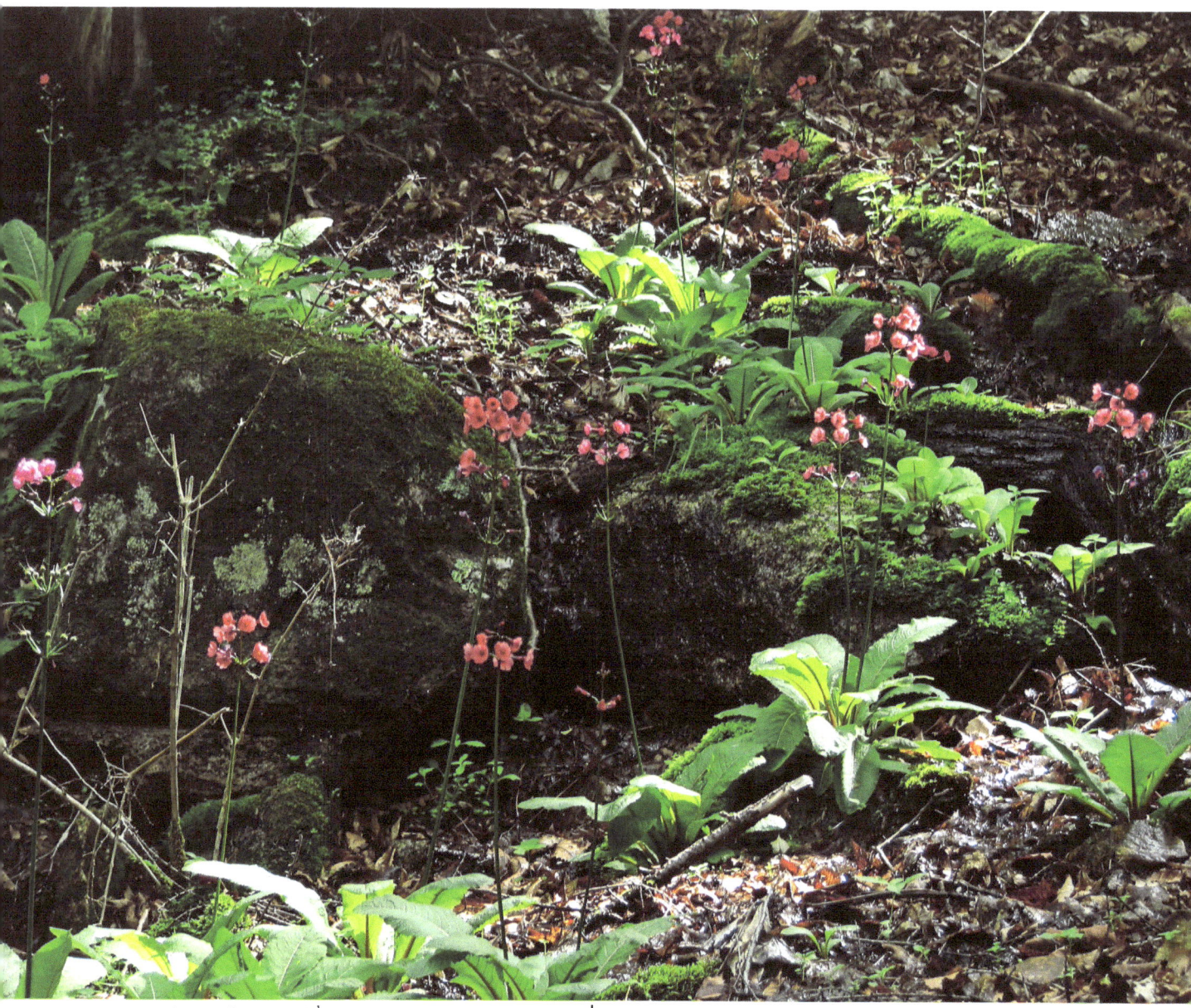

Just above is the 2nd and final shot you'll see of the *Primula japonica*. This photo shows it in an overview so that you can see both the type of place where it is found and also so that you can see just how dark and rather damp it is here in the forest. Look at all of the moss on the rocks and on that one branch on the right side of the photo.

The two photos on the facing page were both taken from a small plateau just about under the arrow which indicates ◄0:40 (40 minutes going this direction). You'll notice (on the map) that there is a very faint line there which indicates an old road which was used at some time in the past. There is a fairly large opening there which afforded us these shots. In the upper photo foreground you can see that it looks like an old road – you can see gravel and what appears to be an old road cut through the rock on the right side of the photo. These photos were both taken at 9:38 AM, about thirty minutes into our hike. Such amazing rock scenery can seldom be seen.

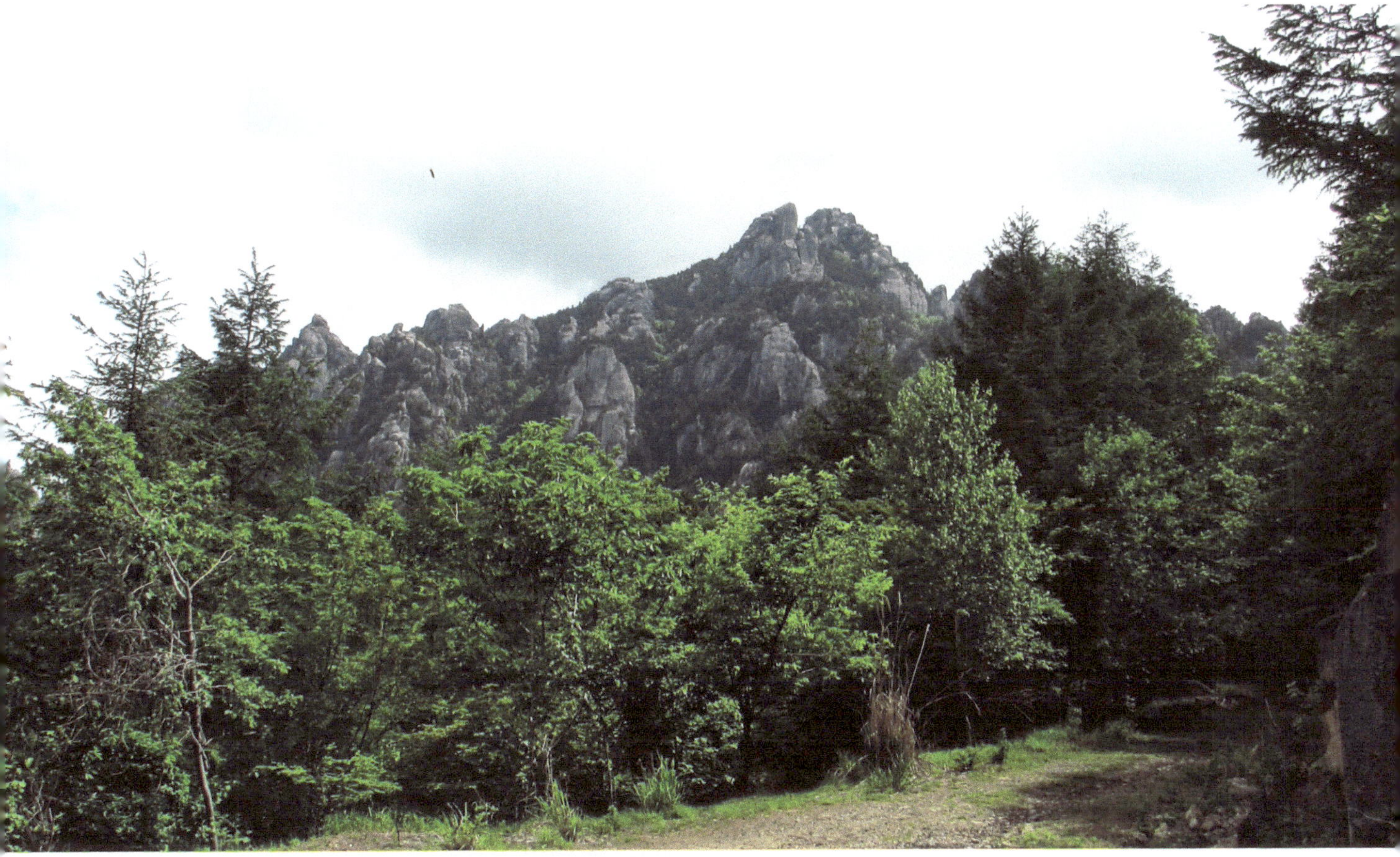

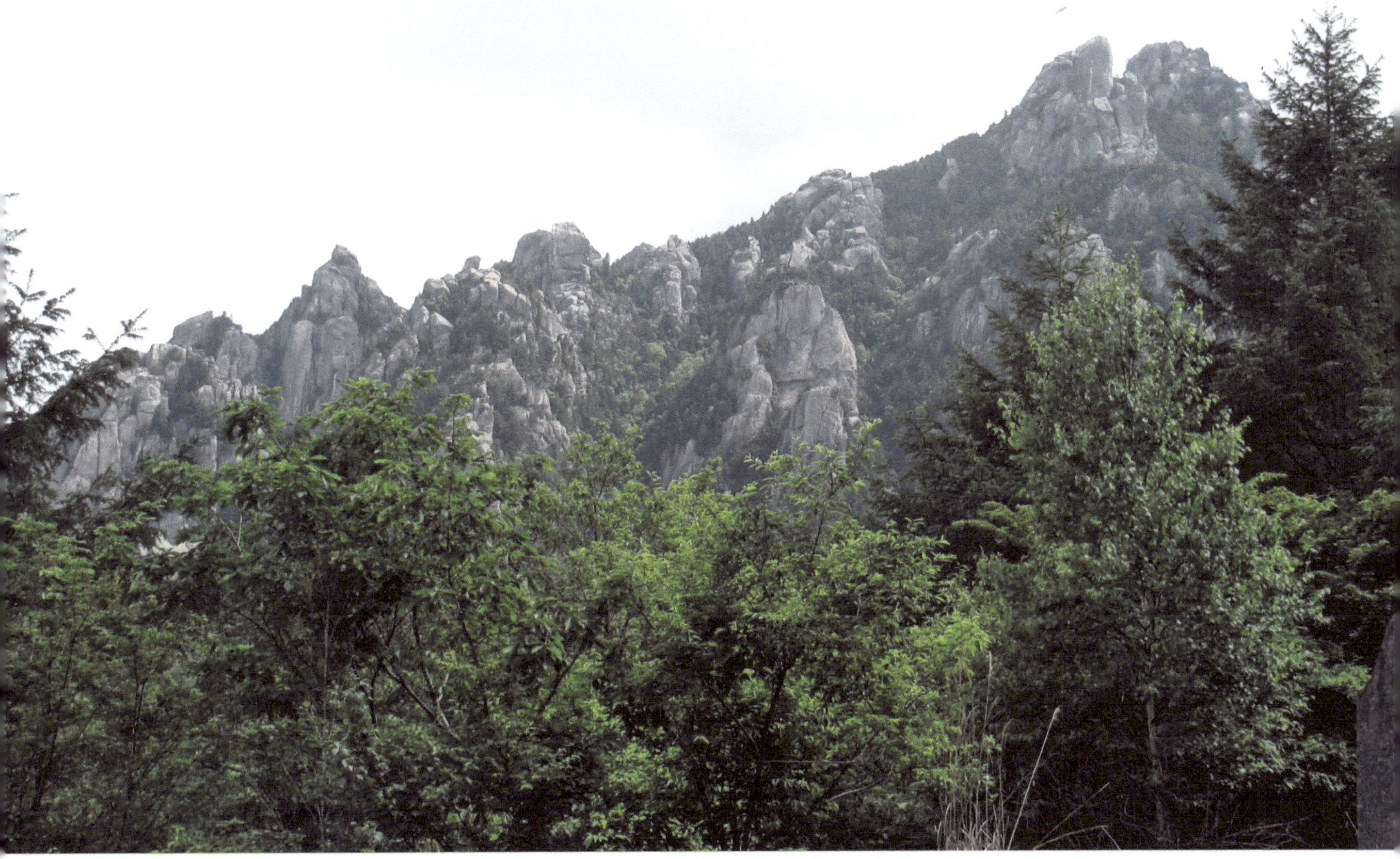

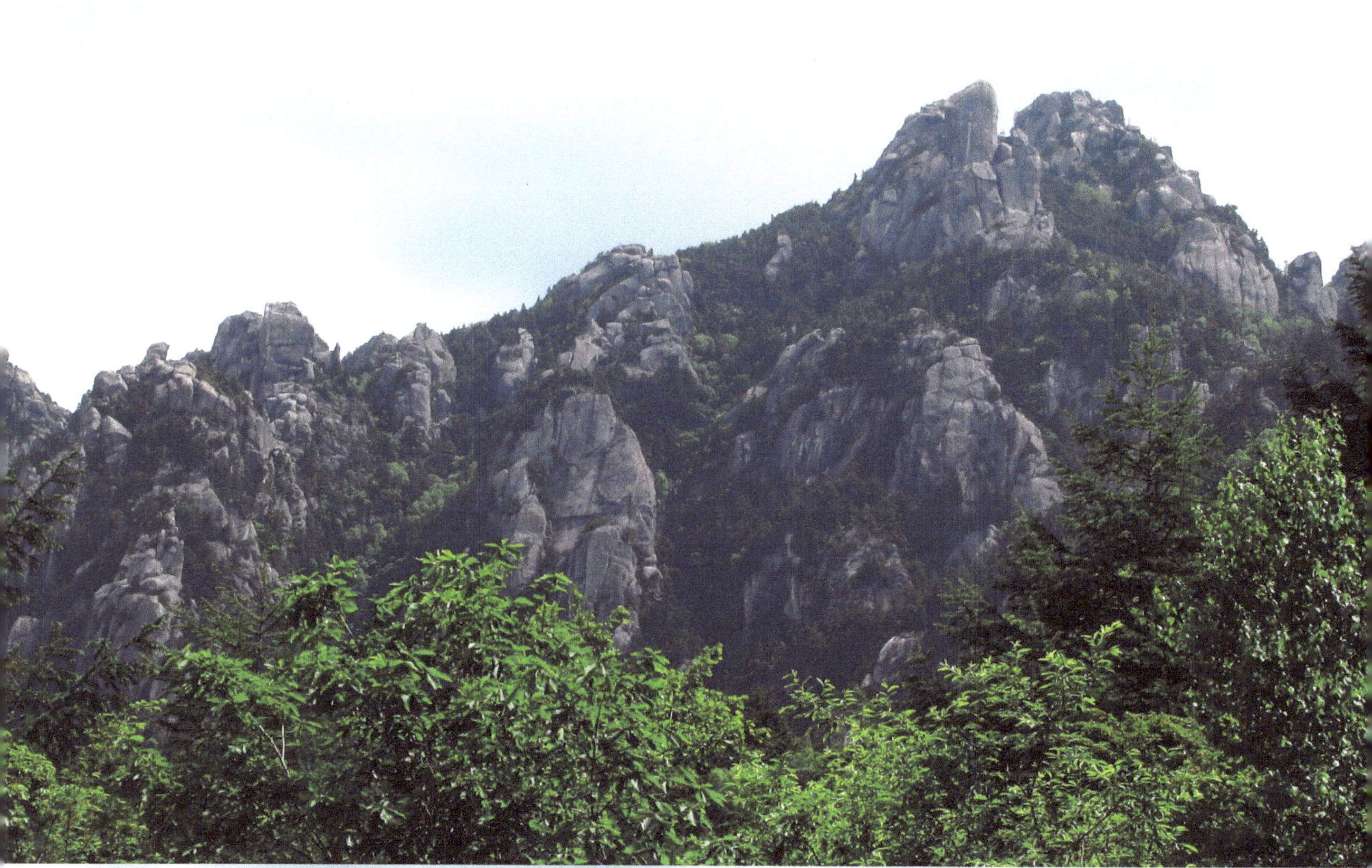

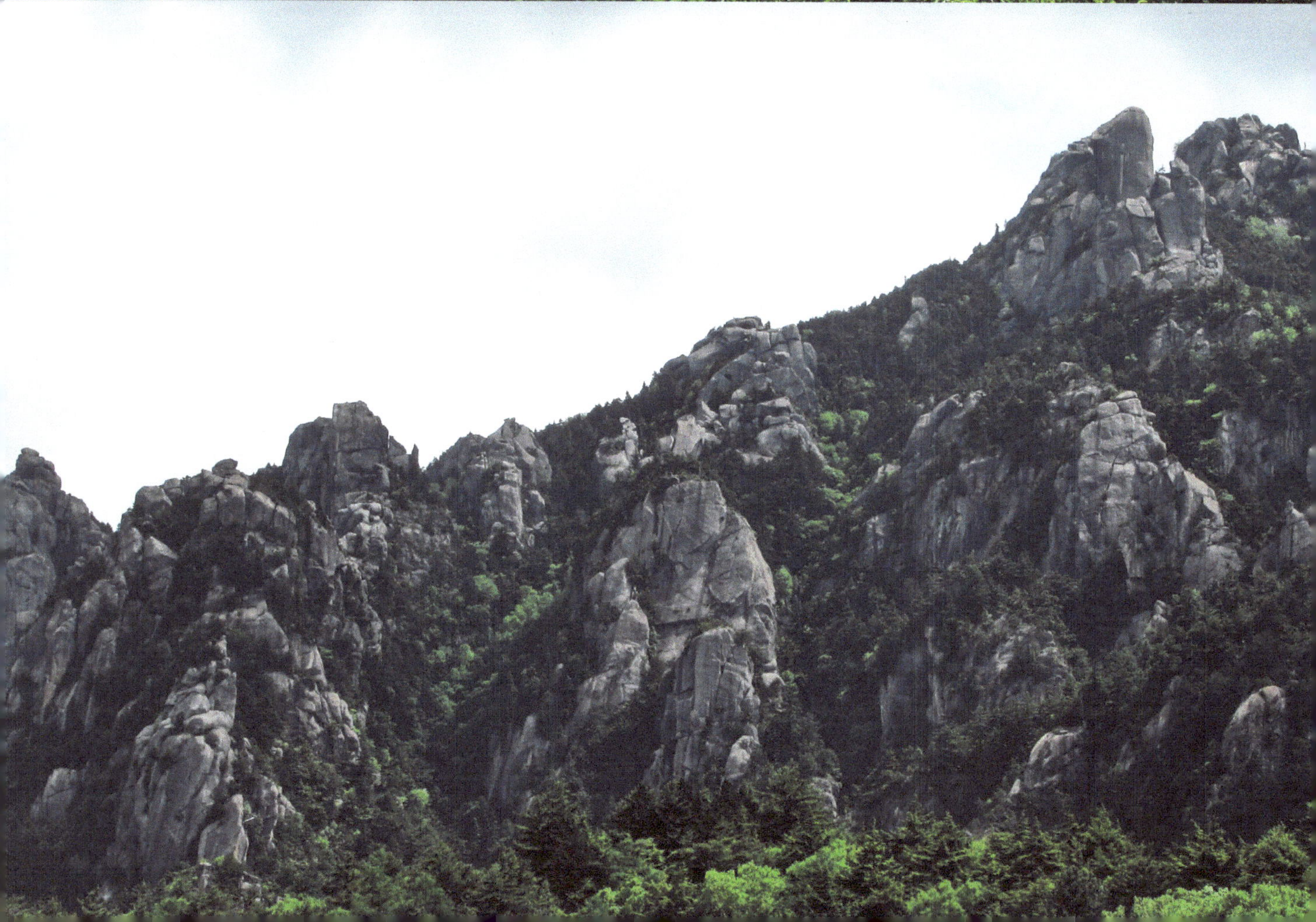

The two facing page photos were taken from approximately the same spot as the previous two photos, however, these two photos were zoomed in more. The upper photo was also taken at 9:38 AM while the lower one was taken at 9:41 AM. We shot an abundance of photos from this general area as it is not often that one can find a clearing like this and have such fantastic views before getting above treeline. We are not sure if any of these shots show the actual summit of the mountain.

The following photo was shot at 9:42 AM and it is zoomed in even more so that you can see this amazing granite rock. Later on we'll show you a photo or two of some people climbing on this mountain, technical climbing that is, with ropes and carabiners and all of the other necessary equipment.

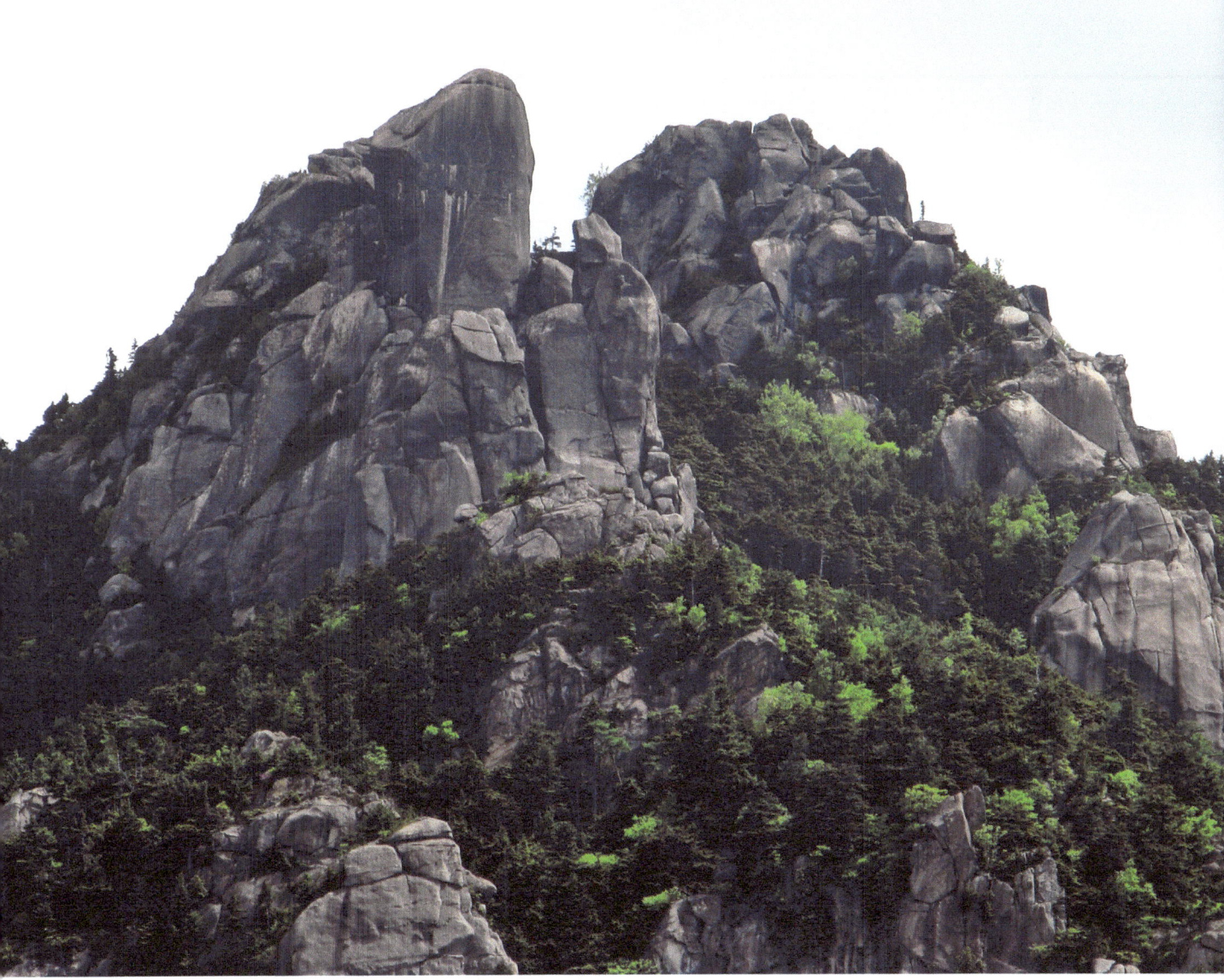

The next photo was zoomed out again and in this photo we are looking off to the left portion of the area shown in the four photos on pages 13 and 14. This shot was taken at 9:42 AM, and although it may appear to you that the area is not as incredibly astounding as the previous photos, we went to call your attention to the lower elevation rock which is near the center of the photo. Okay? Do you see what we're referring to? Take a couple of seconds and study it please.

Why? Now look at the photo on the facing page, which is zoomed in to that rock. Now it really looks quite amazing doesn't it? It has been weathered away in such an interesting way – there are no sharp edges at all.

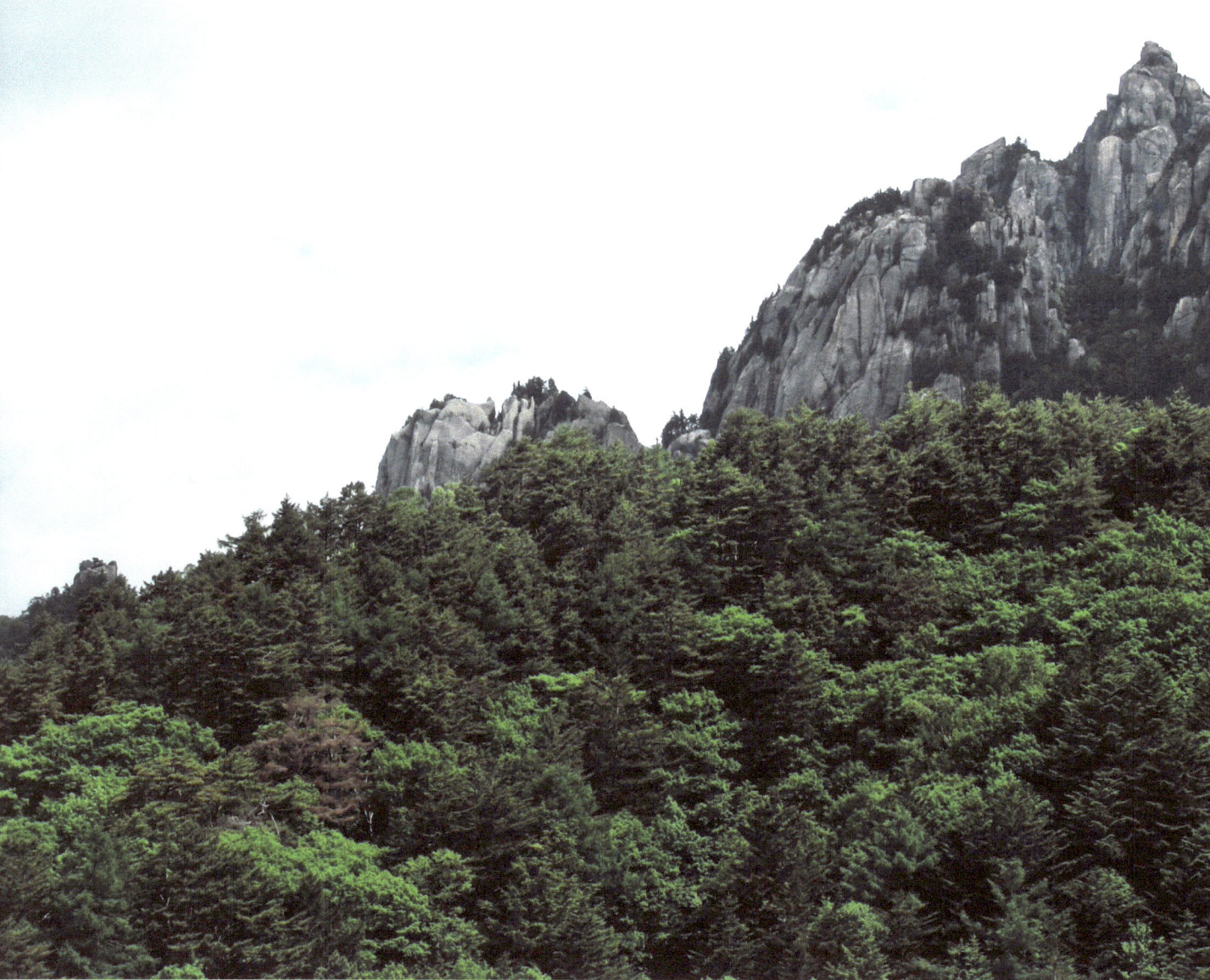

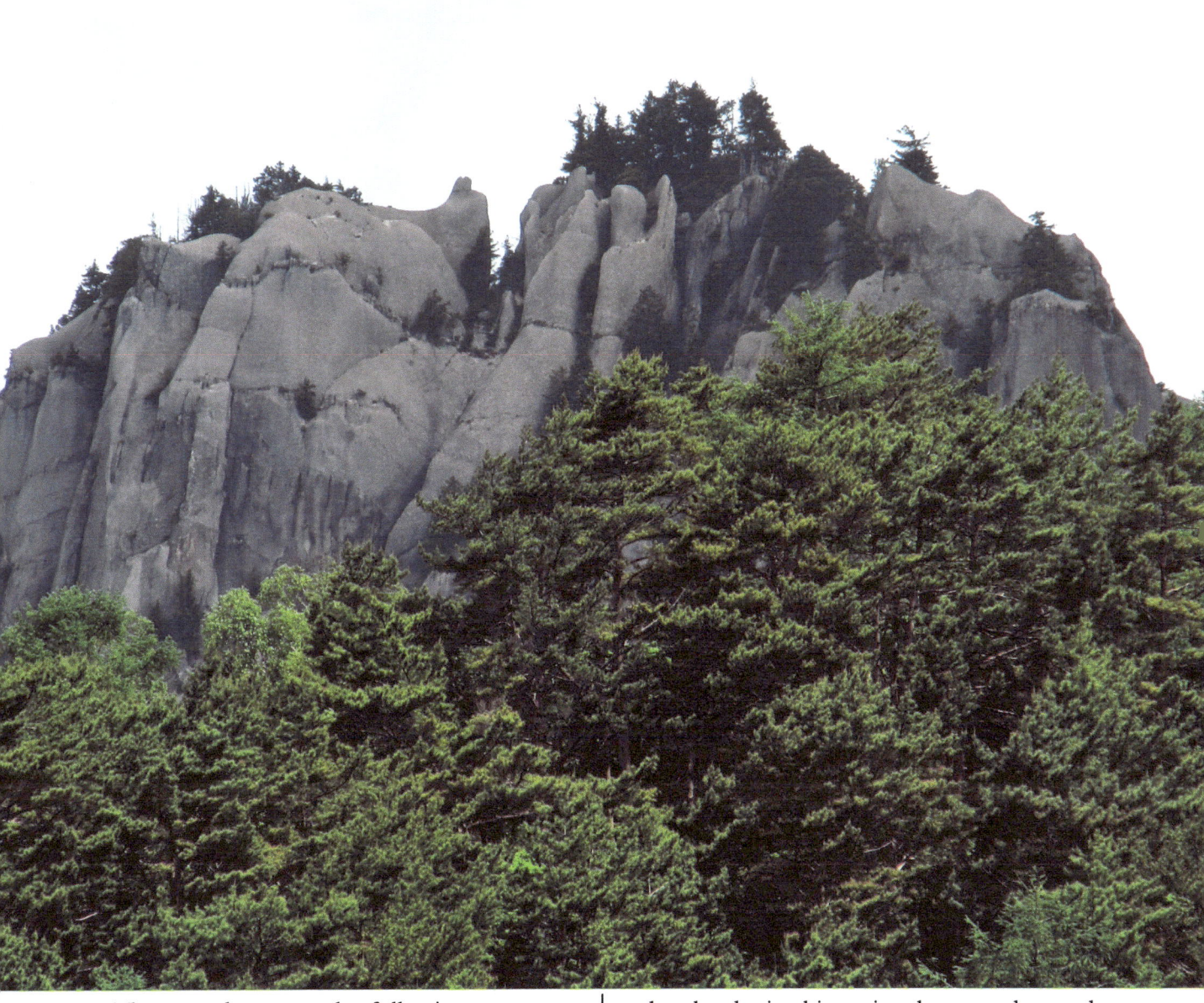

The two photos on the following page were both taken at 9:43 AM and show approximately the same area as some of the previous photos, but in these two photos we have moved to a somewhat different location and have a view which shows more area to the right of the previous photos. The 2nd following photo is a zoomed in shot. This was a unique type of rock formation for us to see. If you have seen other books in this series then you know that this is our first time to see formations of this type. If you continue reading this series you will notice, as we move on to Mt. Shiroumadake, Mt. Tateyama and then, finally, Mt. Yatsugatake that there are no more of this type of rock formations on any other mountains which we have (so far) climbed of Japan's 100 Famous Mountains.

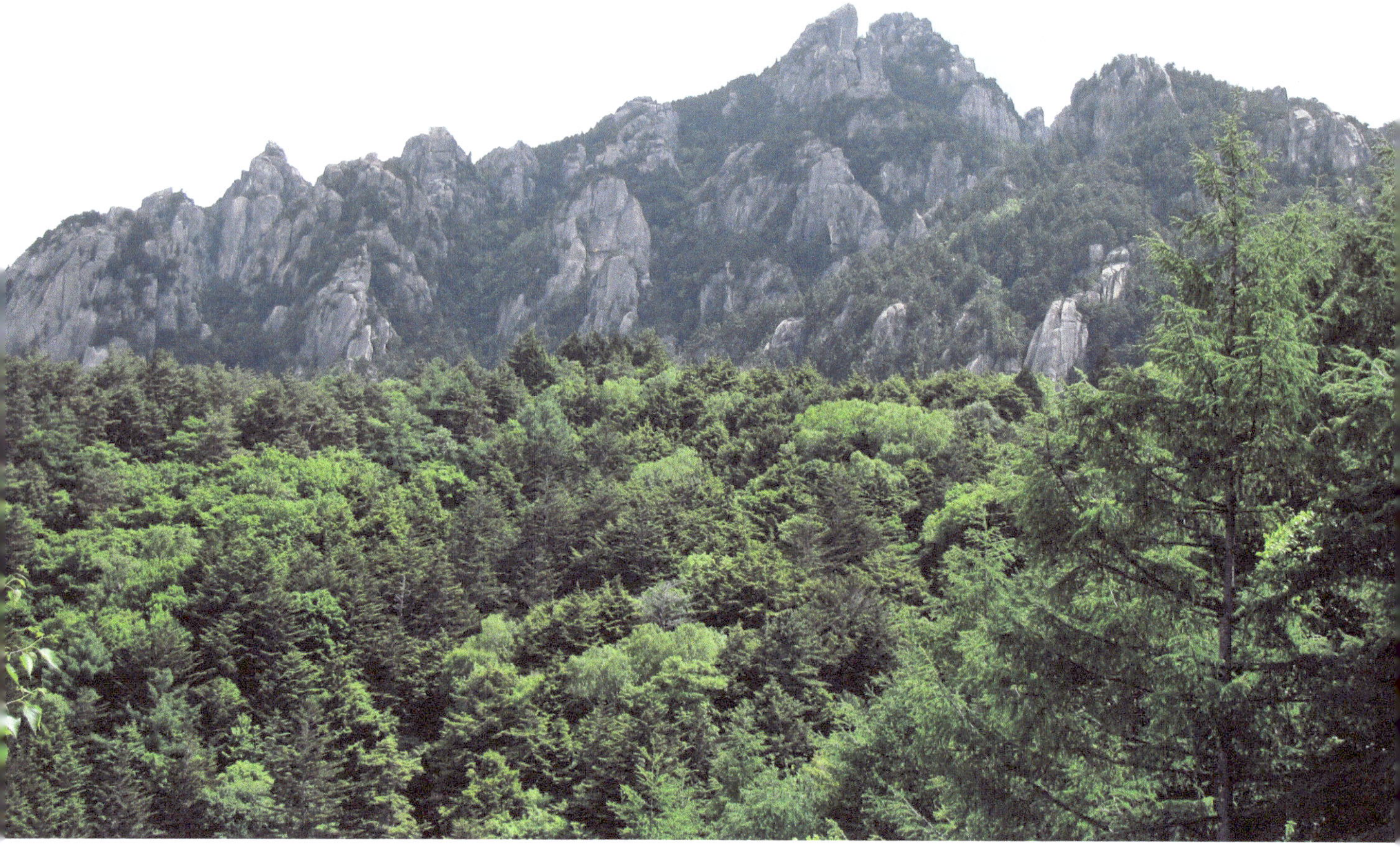
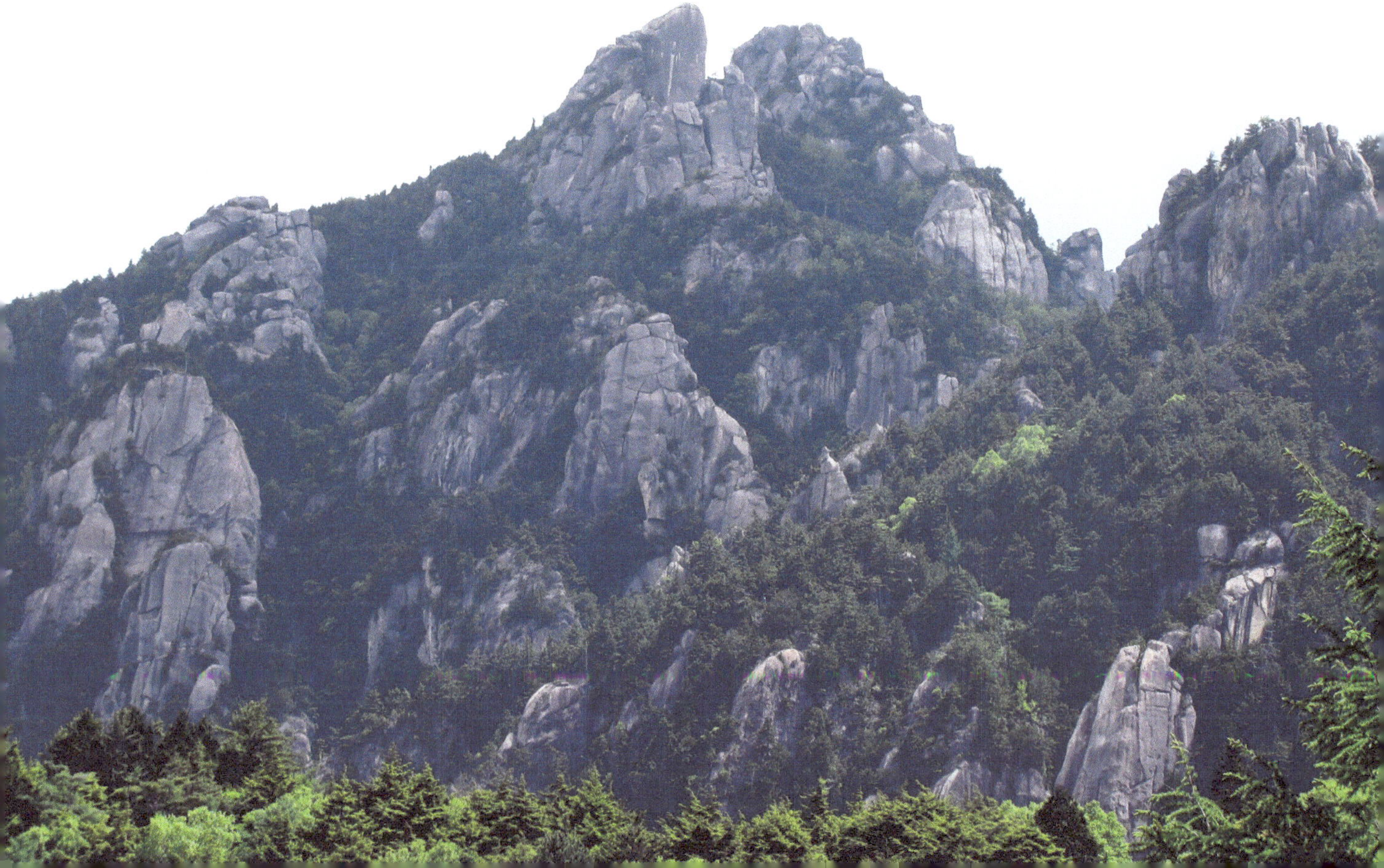

We're sure that you'll notice that the sky is somewhat hazy in all of these photos and that there is little blue sky. Sorry for that, but at least we are not hiking in the clouds on this climb and we do have nice extensive views of our surroundings. One has to keep in mind that this climb was done in June, which is traditionally Japan's rainy season, so we were just extremely happy that it was not raining.

The following photo is one of the Fuji-mi-daira-koya Hut (富士見平小屋), the 2) annotation on the map on page 9. The time was 10:19 AM, so it took us about one hour and ten minutes to get here from the bus stop. You may notice that the map indicates that the hike from the bus stop to this hut should be fifty minutes. We never (or seldom) are able to climb as fast as the maps indicate and we like to think that this is due to the fact that we stop to take too many photographs. Please recall from page 8 that we also were scouring the area for a specific species of orchid which was reported as being in bloom just a few days prior to this climb.

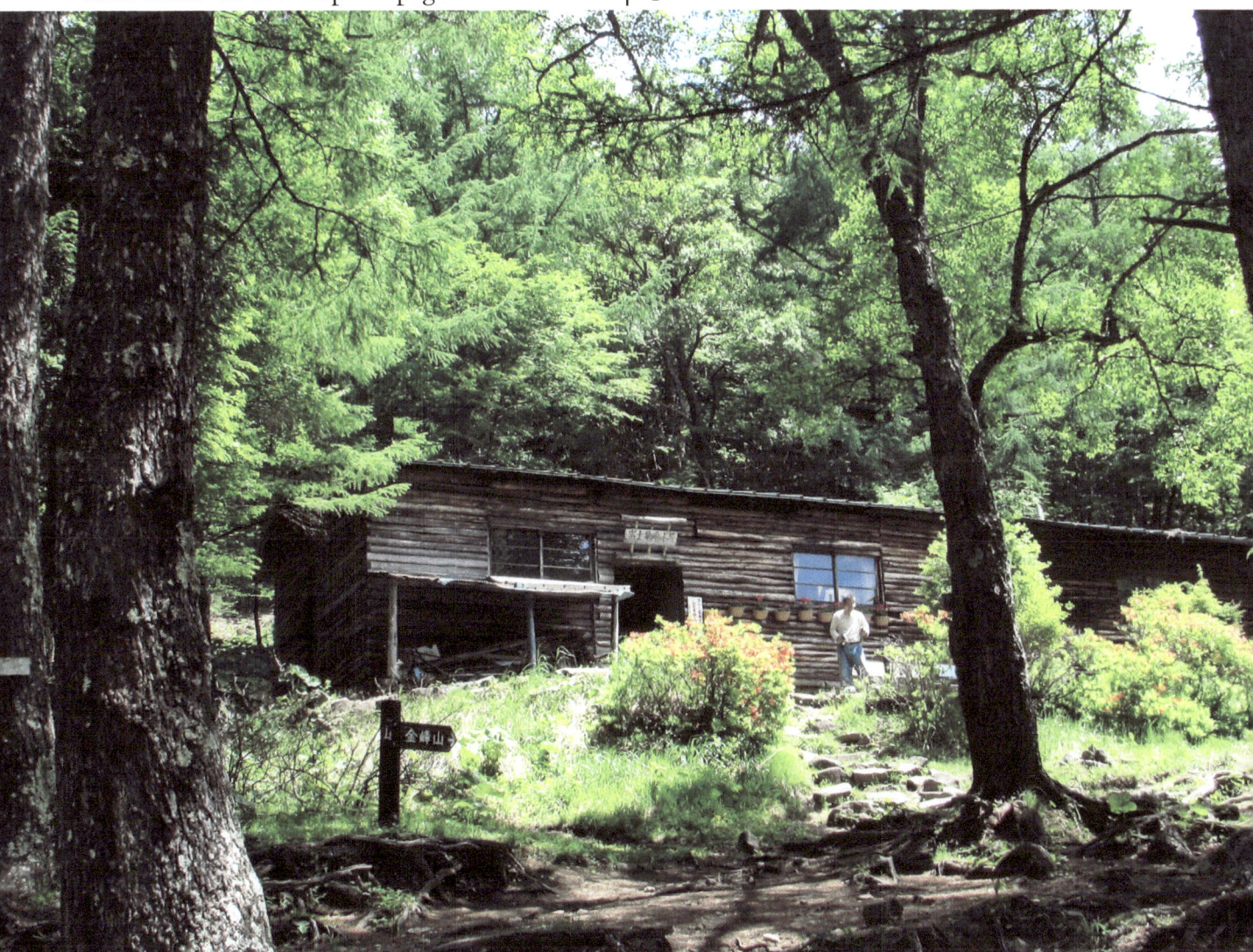

The sign in front of this hut points the way to Mt. Kinpu (to the right). There is a water source here so you should fill your water bottles here if you need to, as there are no additional water sources between here and the summit of Mt. Mizugaki.

The next photo, just below, was taken at 10:36 AM and shows some rocks which are new, that is, we have not yet seen them. We have now passed the hut and we are following the trail marked with the 3) annotation on the map on page 9. As we approached closer to the pillar which is on the left in this photo we witnessed some people climbing it. We'll show you some of those photos later on, when we get closer.

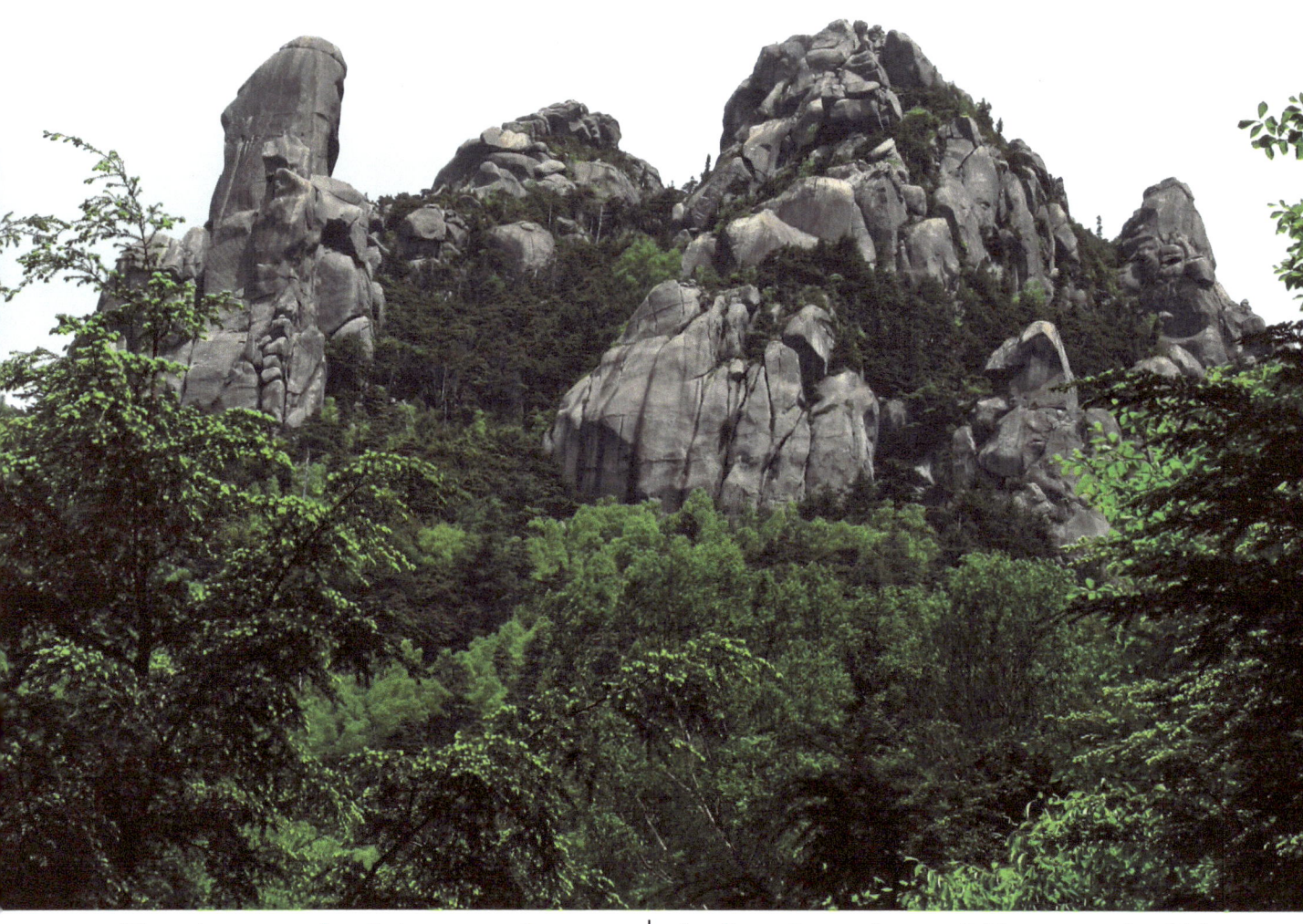

The photo on the facing page shows an interesting huge rock which has been split by the elements, or maybe it split when it fell here from somewhere a few millennia ago. One thing that you should notice here is all of the sticks and poles which people have jokingly placed here as props to prevent this rock from rolling. This is the first of two photos of this same rock which we'll show you, and the only rock we'll show you which has these props under it, but we witnessed these props placed under the leading edges of many huge rocks as we ascended. We did not add any props to those already in place, but we were tempted to do so.

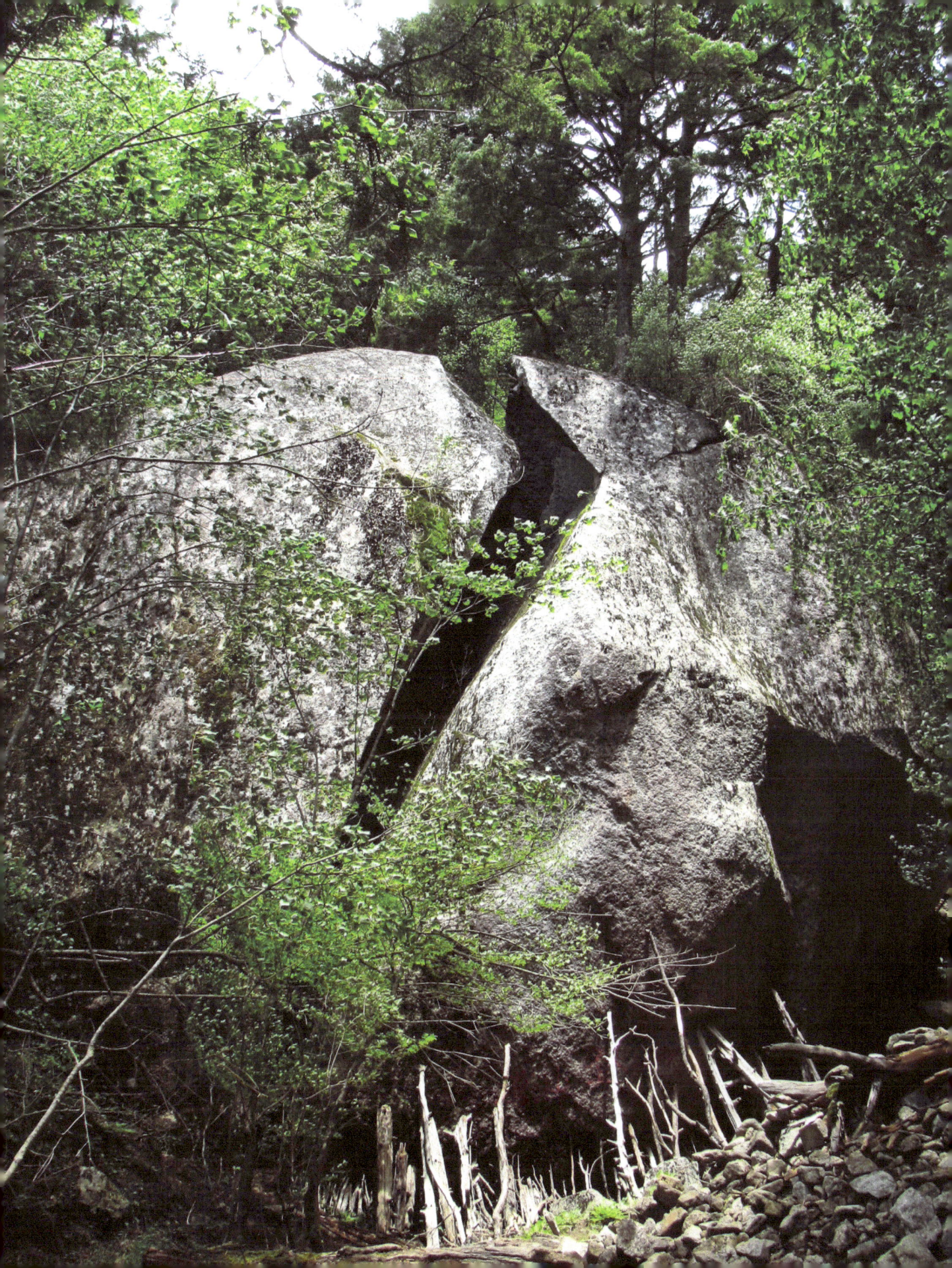

The next photo shows the same rock, as just shown, but this one was taken in landscape mode at 10:49 AM. In our opinion this photo gives a somehow better idea of the scale, what do you think? We suppose that the very best indicator for the scale, using 20/20 hindsight, would have been if one of us had gone and stood in the photo. Just to give you an idea though, this rock must be at least 7 meters (= 23 ft) high.

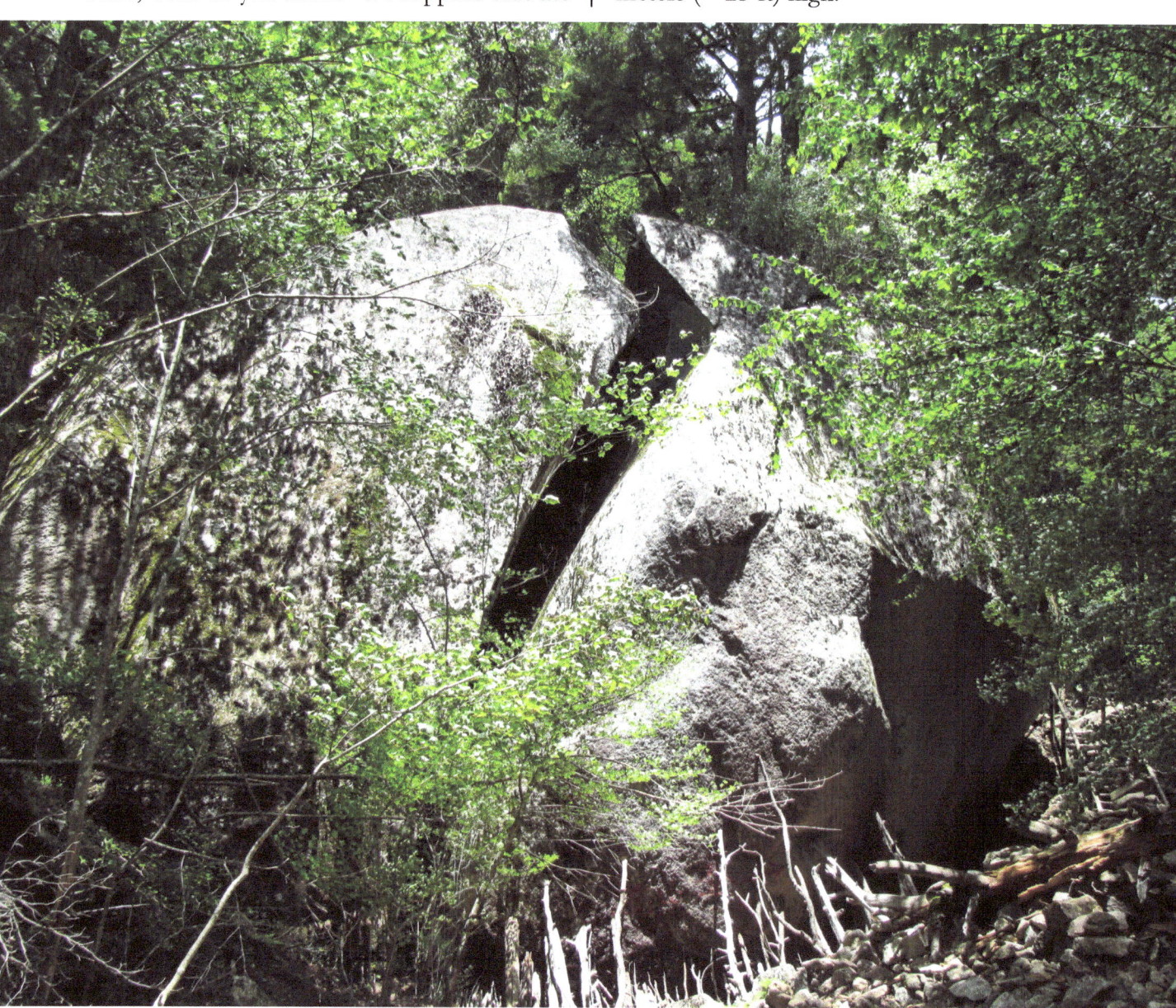

The next two photos are both full page spreads. The first one, on the facing page, is looking up the trail and shows me at 11:37 AM (about forty-five minutes before we reached the summit). The second one is looking down the trail and shows Kazuya. You should note how very rocky it is and that there is very little underbrush growing here.

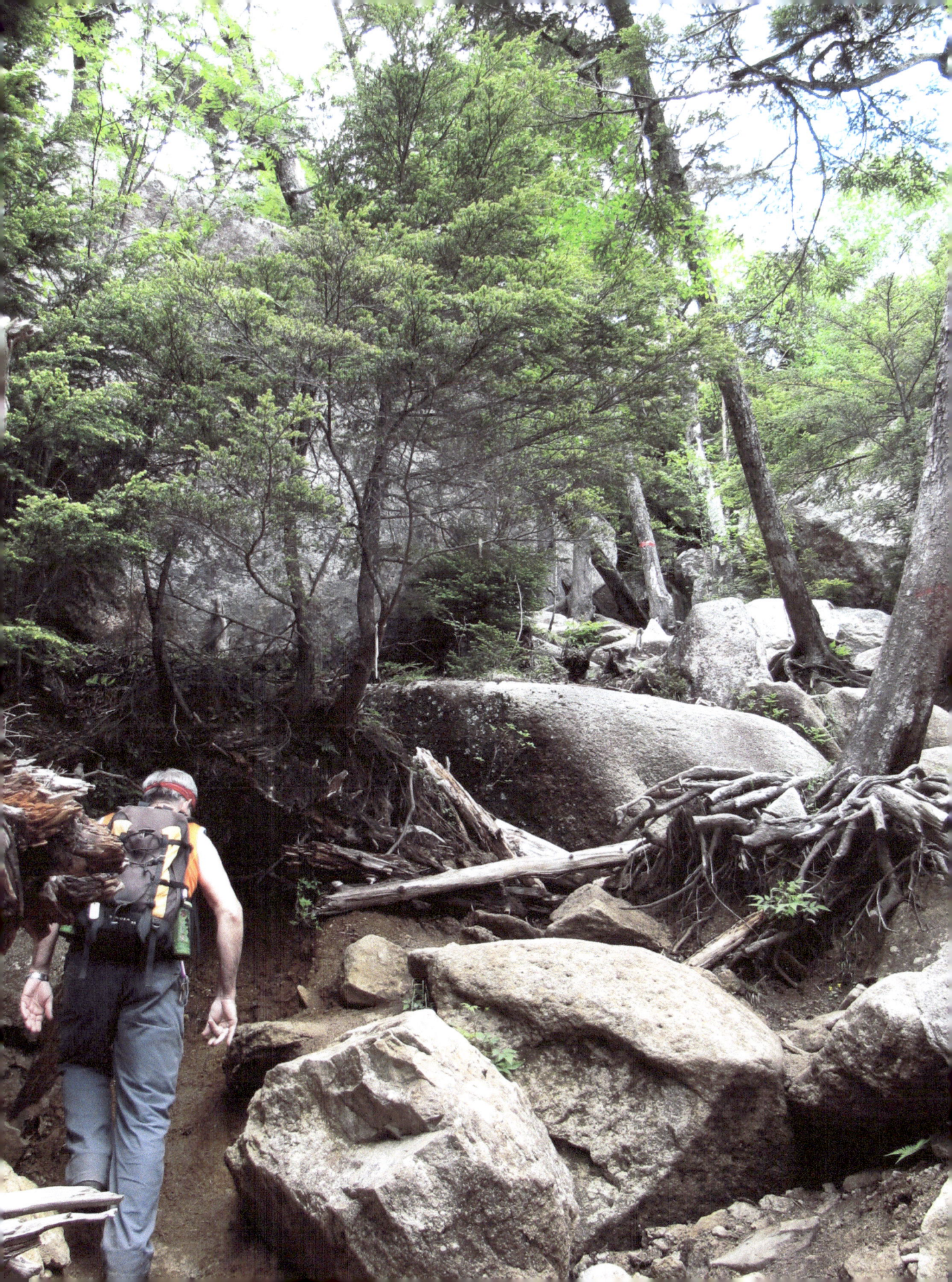

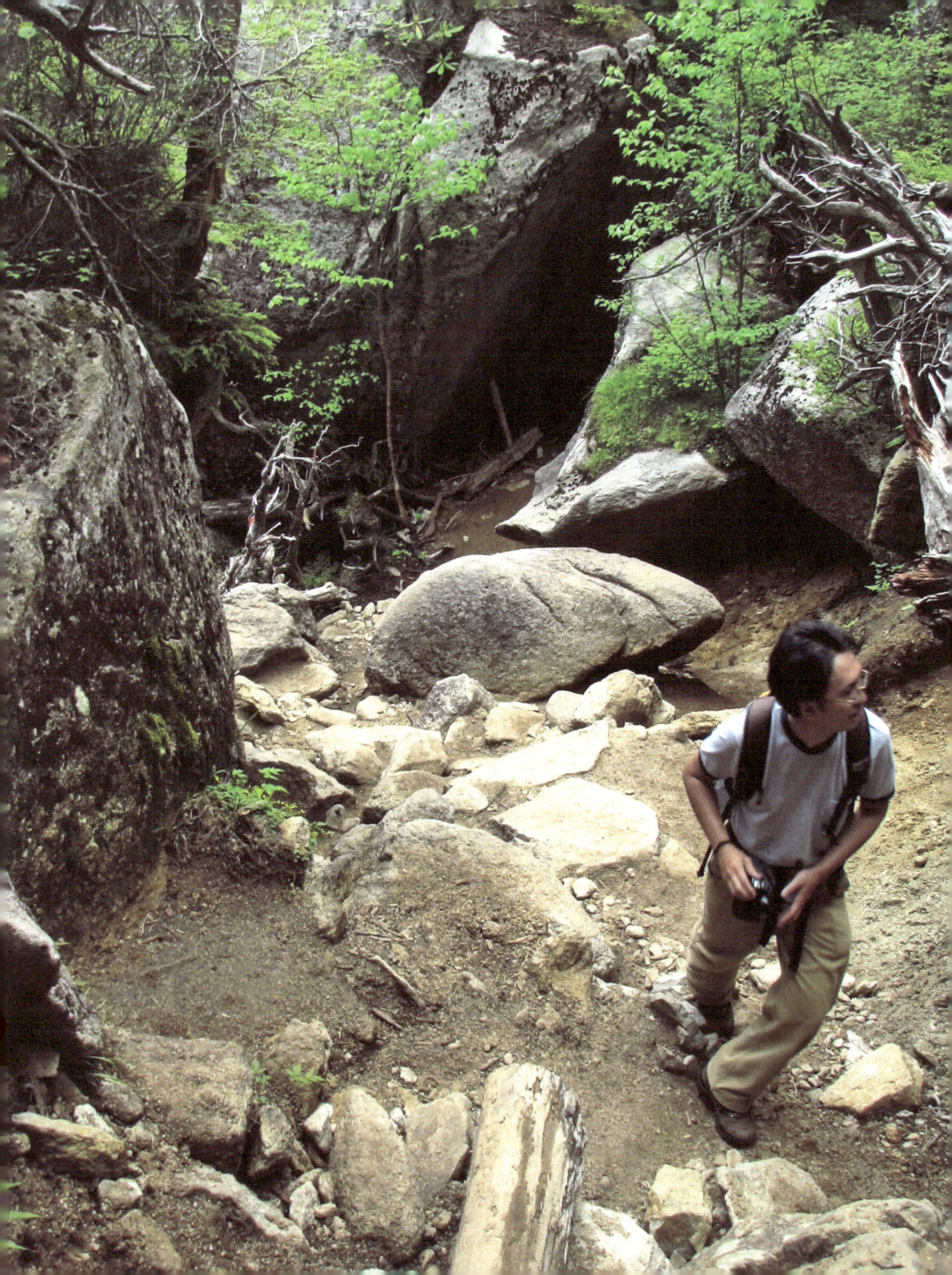

In the following photo you may recognize the rock and the piece of red flagging on the tree from the photo on page 23. This photo shows the colors very nicely and also shows just how rock strewn this trail is. This photo was also taken at 11:37 AM.

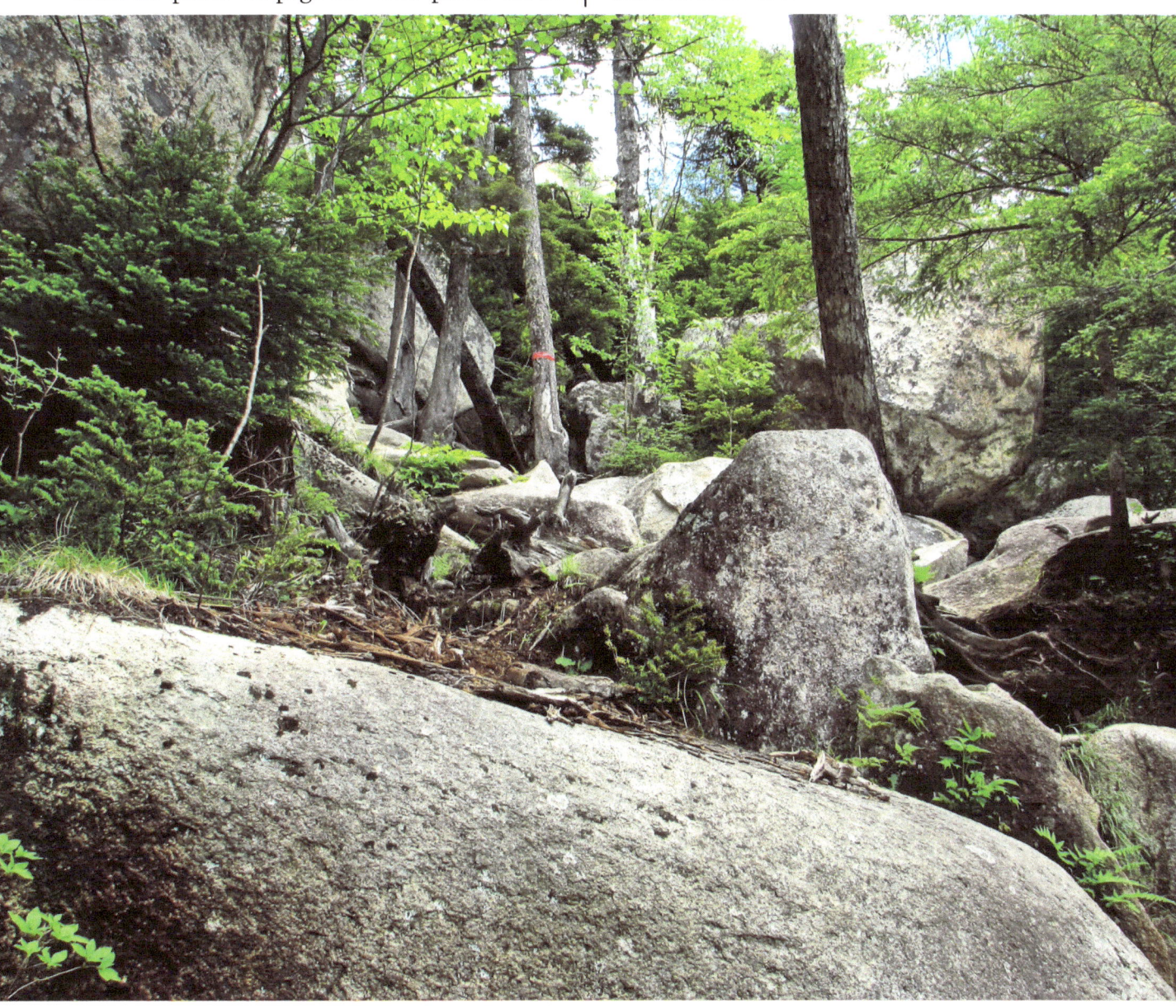

The next photo is again a full page spread and shows another rock pillar which we have not yet shown you. It was taken at 11:41 AM, so we are still about forty minutes below the summit. If you study the photo a bit you can see a rope and a red flag on the rope. The rock in the lower right corner also has a large red "X" on it (which you can see a portion of), the rope with the red flag and the red "X" are both indications that one should not attempt to go this way. It's a pretty amazing rock, wouldn't you agree?

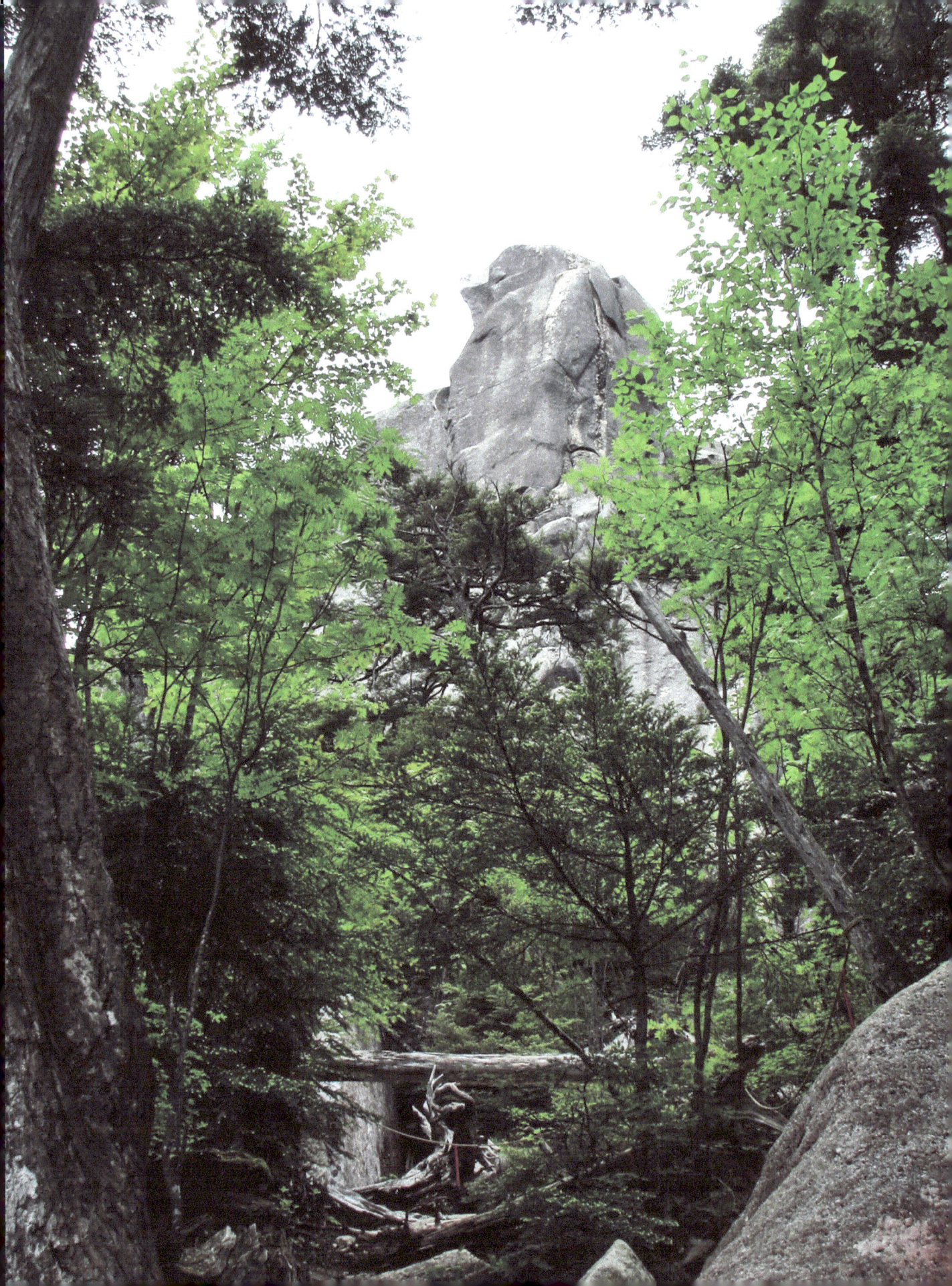

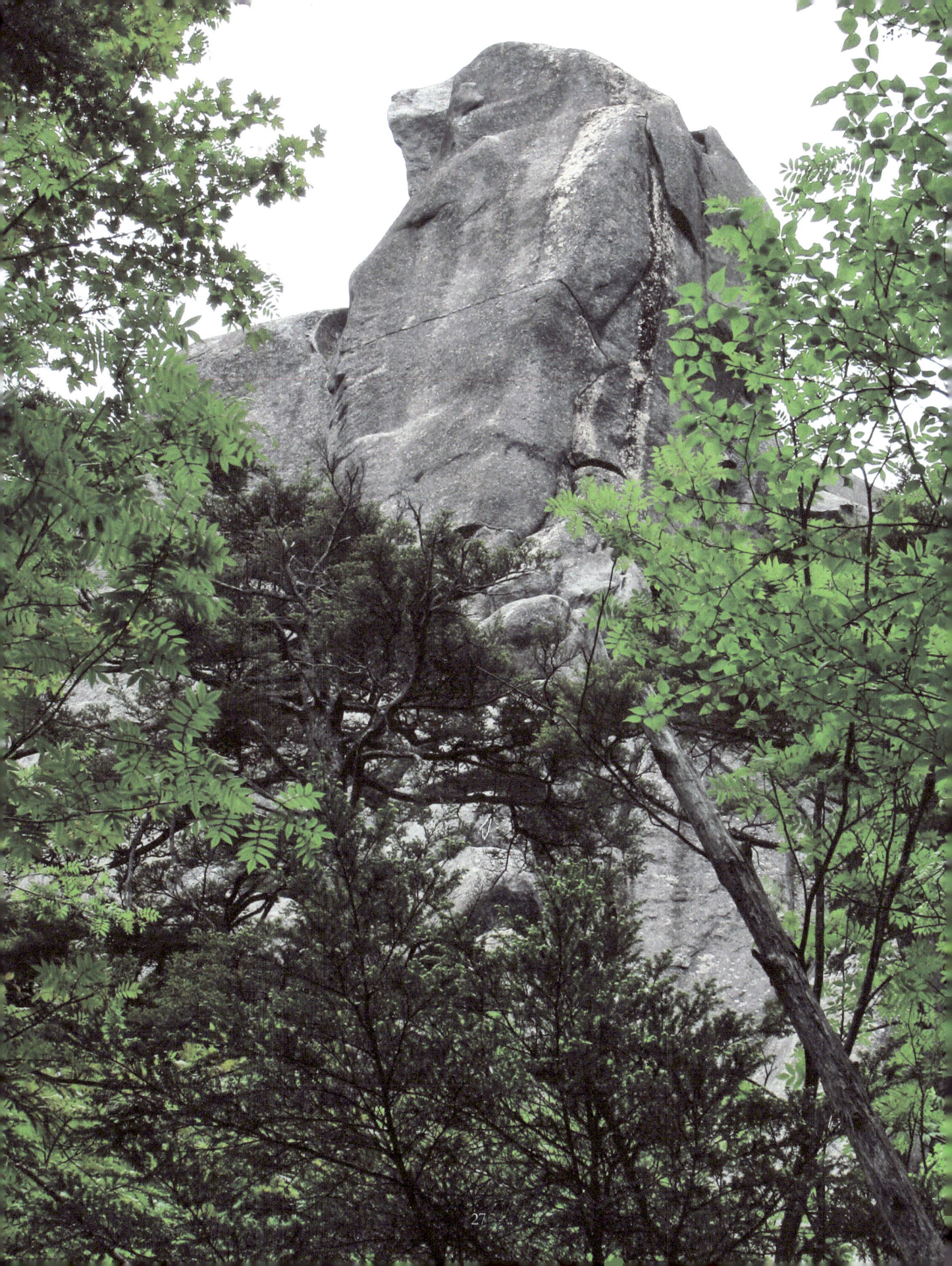

The previous photo is zoomed in to show a closer view of the same rock which was shown in the photo before it (page 26).

The following photo is, of course, of Mt. Fuji. The dead tree snag on the left makes for a nice frame, at least on that side. You can see that, although there are clouds in the sky, we have a pretty good view of our surroundings. Hopefully the weather will not deteriorate and change to rain.

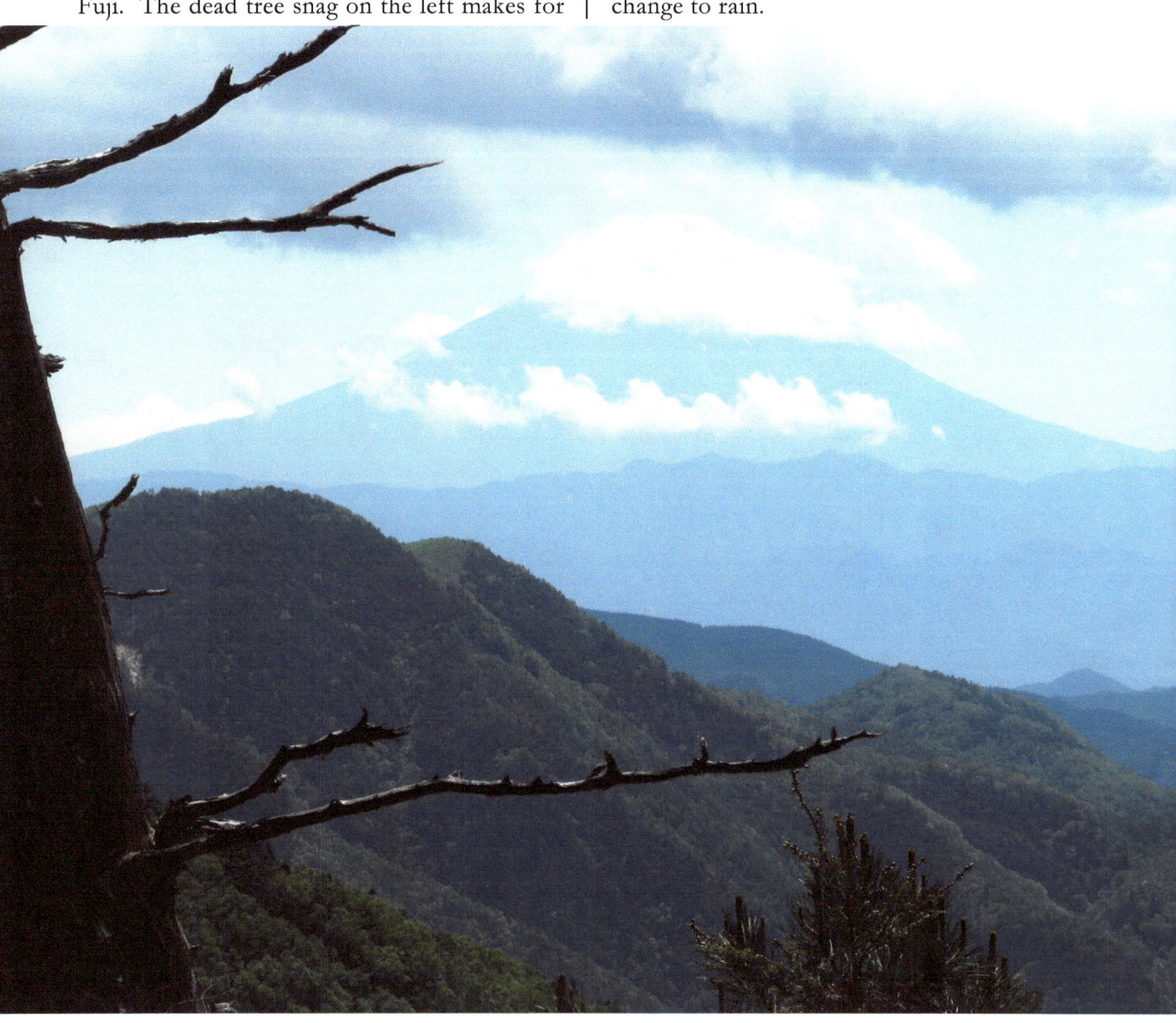

The facing page photo shows the same rock which was shown on page 26 and also on page 27, but it was taken from a different spot along the trail, and therefore from a different angle.

Having been an amateur technical climber (very amateur) when I was a young man, this looks so very intriguing to me. If I was still young I would have been very excited about it.

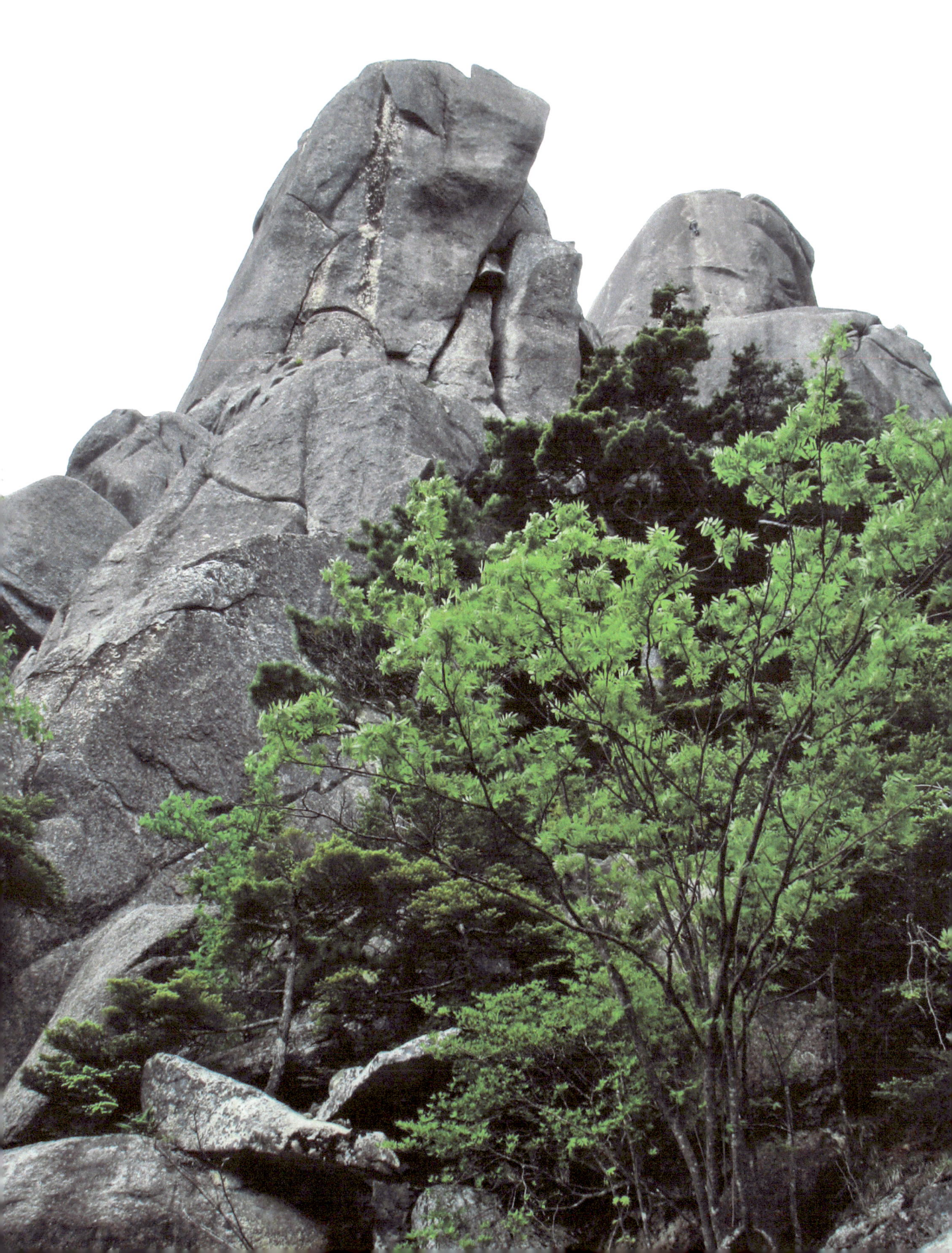

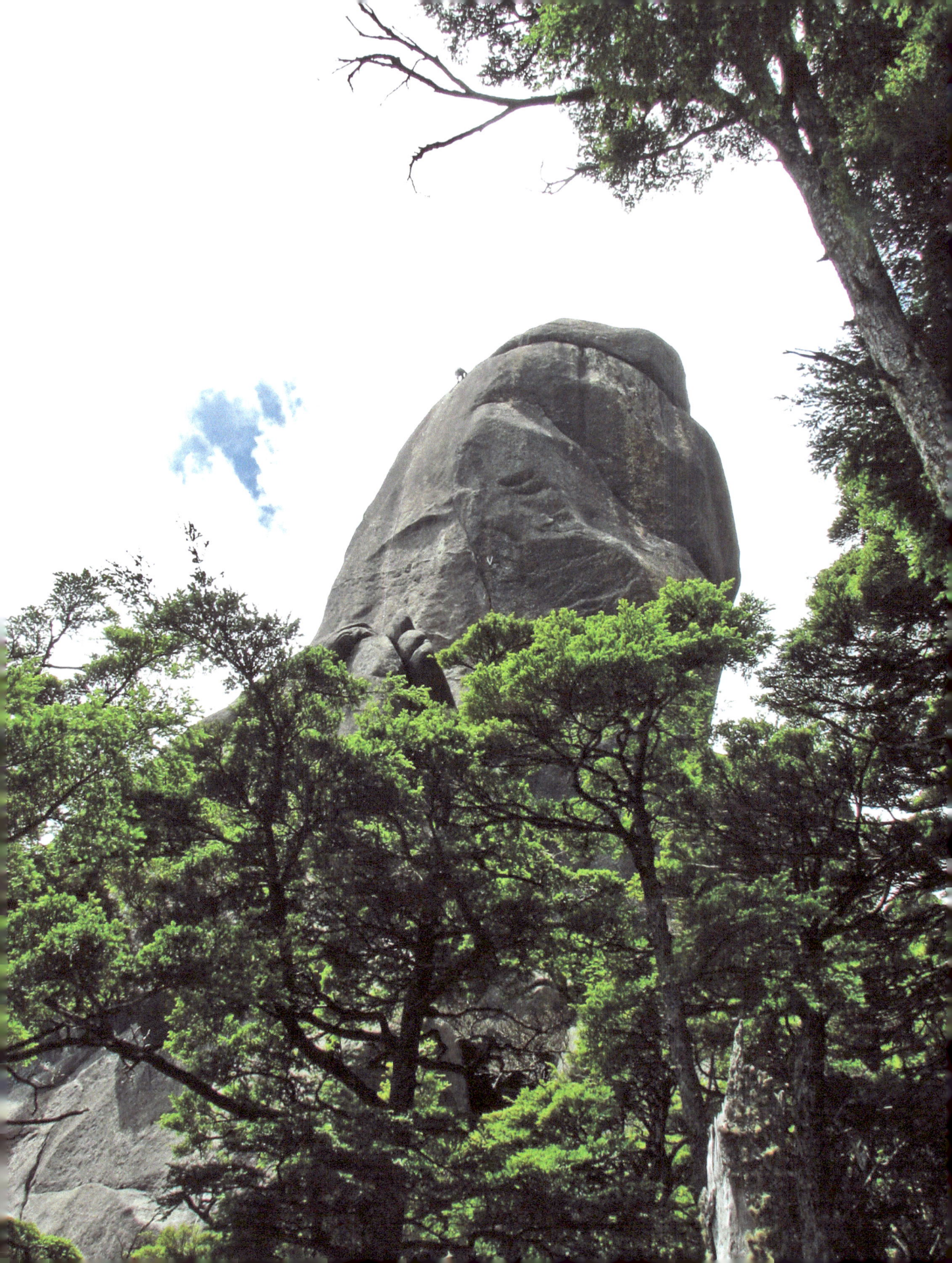

The facing page photo shows a different rock pillar than the one shown on the previous pages and on this one you can see a climber. Amazing! This photo was taken at 11:56 AM, still about twenty-five minutes below the summit.

The following photo shows the same rock and the same climber as shown in the previous photo. This one, however is more zoomed in then the previous photo. It appears that there are no cracks or handholds on this face.

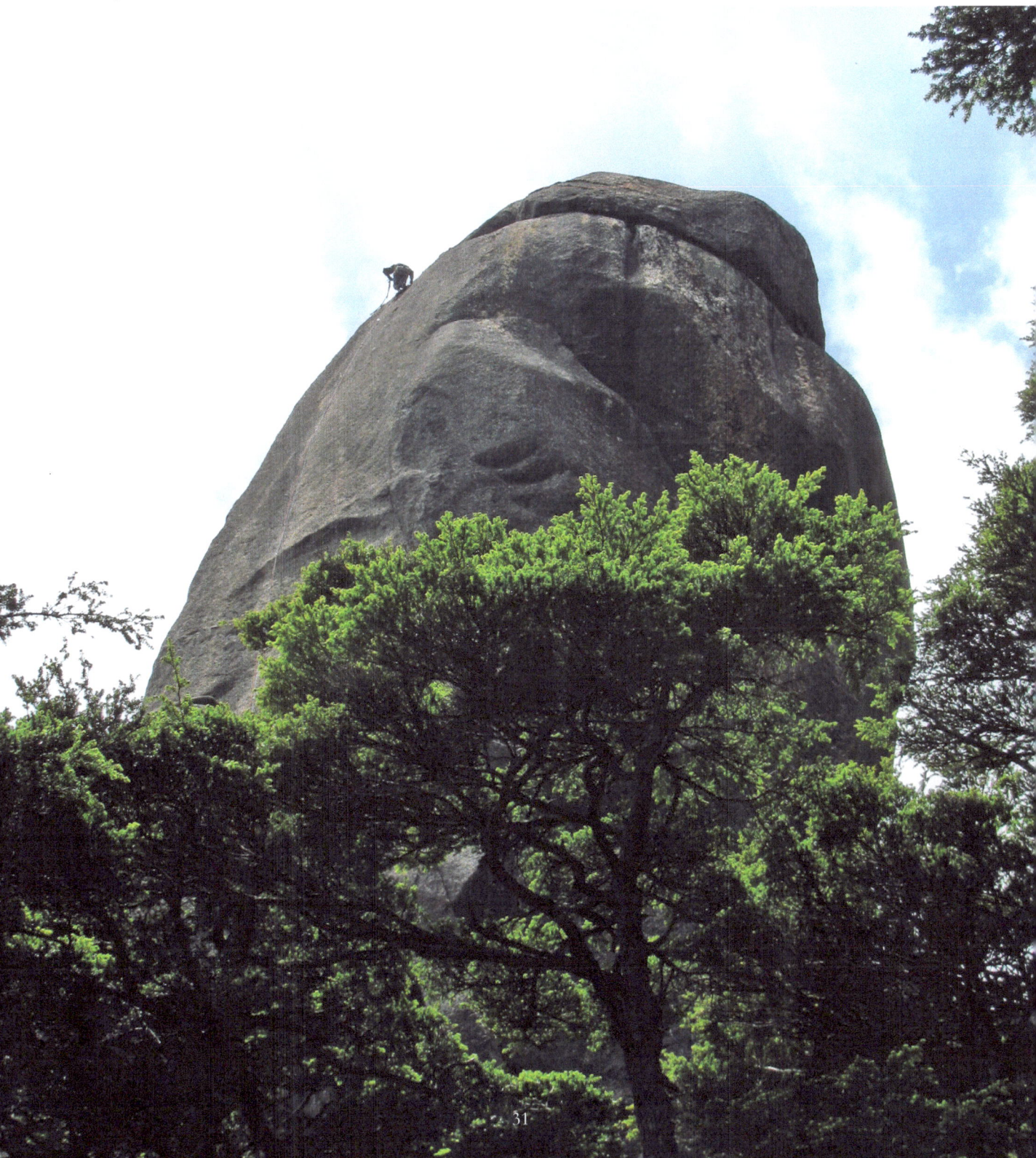

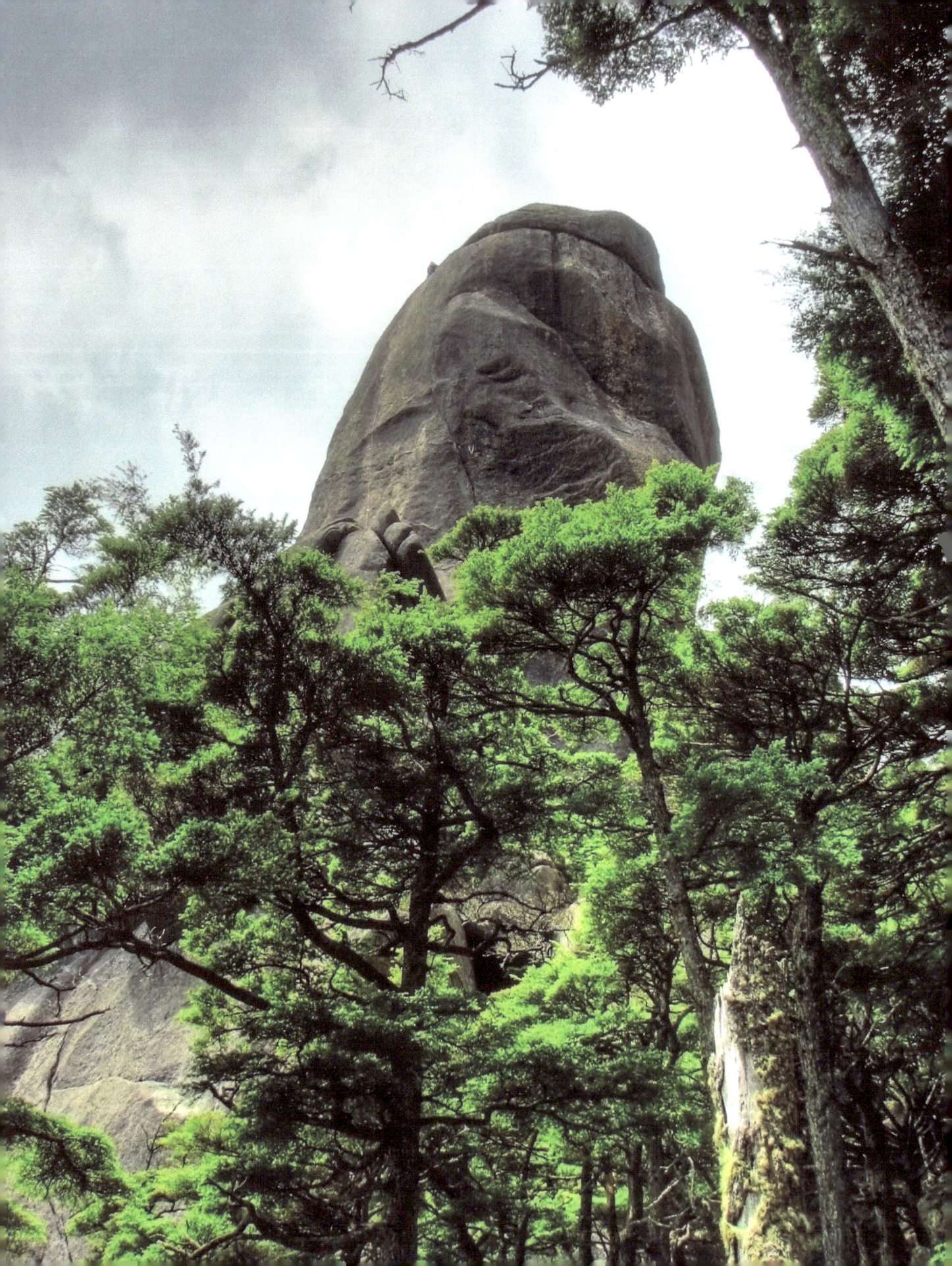

The facing page image is what is called an HDR photo – that is **H**igh **D**ynamic **R**ange. HDR photos are created using special software by combining three or more exposure-bracketed photos of the same scene. That means that you have to be careful to hold the camera in precisely the same position while taking three photos with different exposure settings. The software is clever enough so that it can match features as long as you can hold the camera relatively stable while shooting. My camera has an exposure-bracketing setting, so I can just use that and it is easier to hold the camera relatively steady – just get myself into a stable position, point and shoot. These HDR photos are very difficult to manipulate in a manner so that they look truly natural, and we are sure that you noticed this in the above image – it's nice, but it looks fake.

Let us show you what the original three photos looked like.

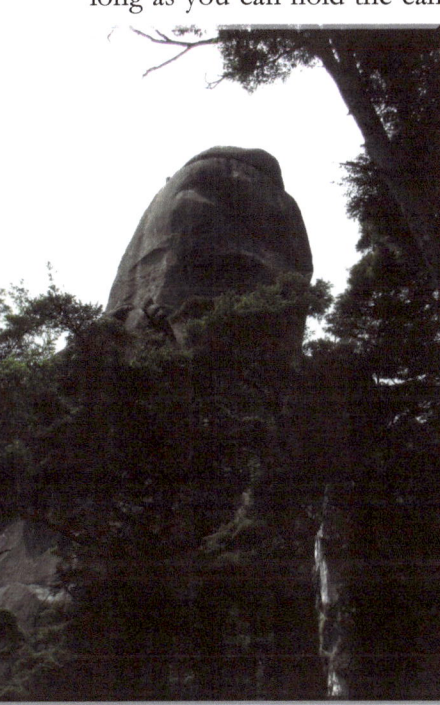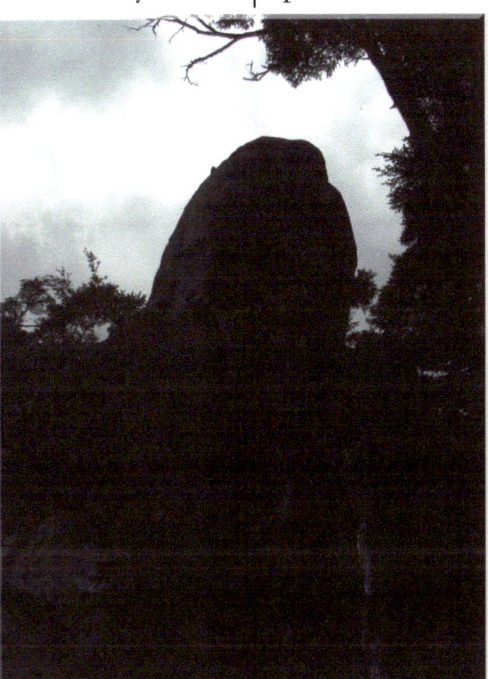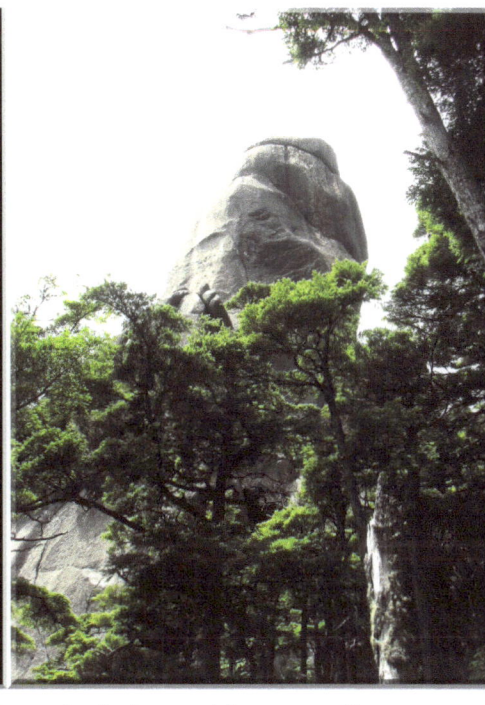

The left photo was taken at what the camera considered the best exposure for this scene. Due to the bright sky and the shade on the rocks and in the forest, the sky is washed out and the foreground is so dark that the photo is pretty much garbage! The center photo was shot at one full f-stop below what the camera considered best exposure. The sky now shows up nicely, but everything else is garbage. The right photo was shot at one full f-stop above what the camera considered to be the best exposure. Now the sky is garbage, but the foreground is fairly good. The software puts all of the photos together and allows you to do some additional manipulation. After spending several minutes of going through all of that, the results are as shown in the HDR photo shown on the facing page. Interesting, no?

The photo on the following page was shot at 12:08 PM, about twenty minutes below the summit. It shows the same rock pillar as shown in the previous few photos, but we have moved higher up the mountain, so we are about at the same level as the top of this pillar at this point. In this photo you can see two climbers if you study it closely. A full-size image of each climber is also shown so that you can easily find them.

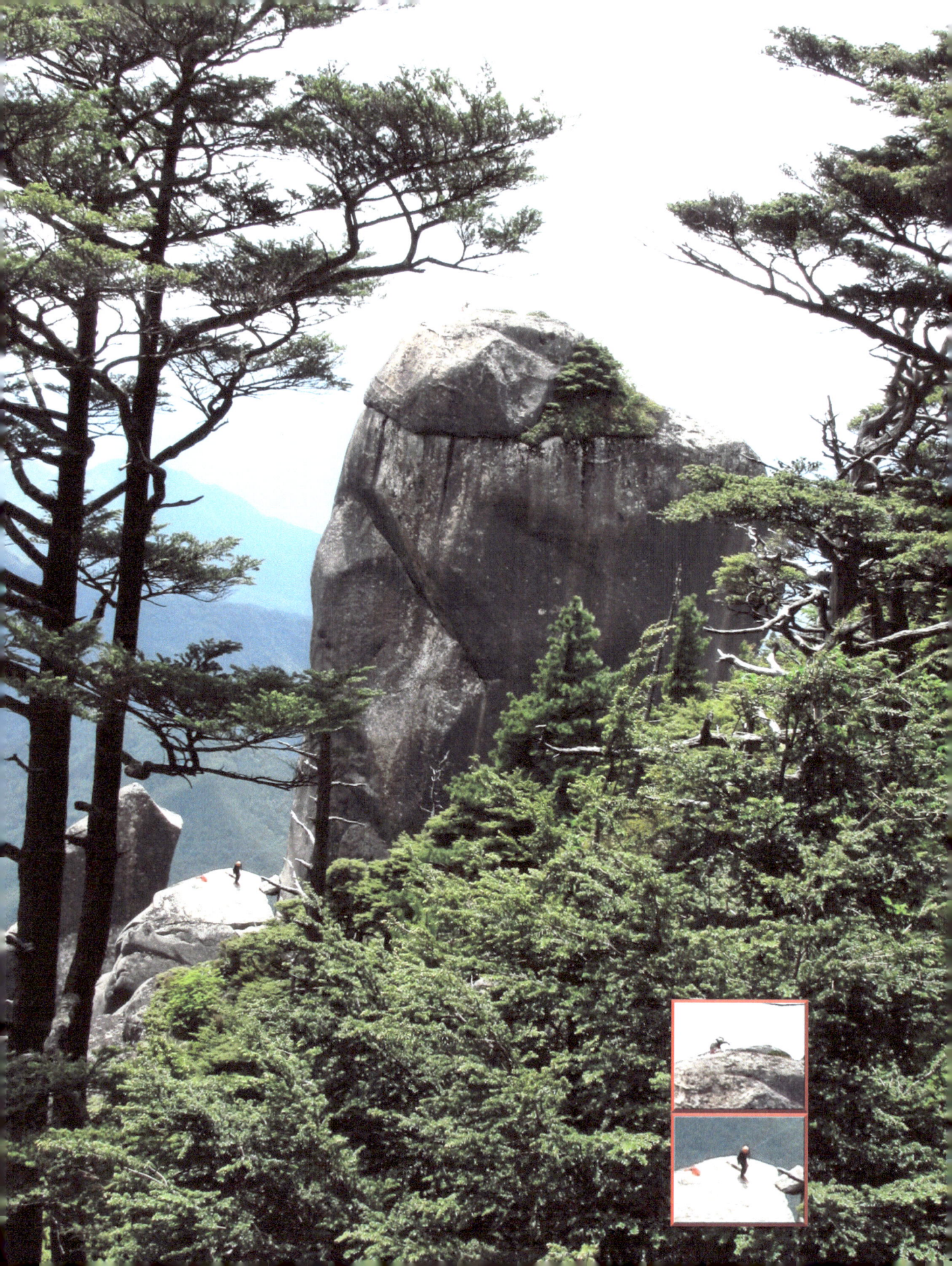

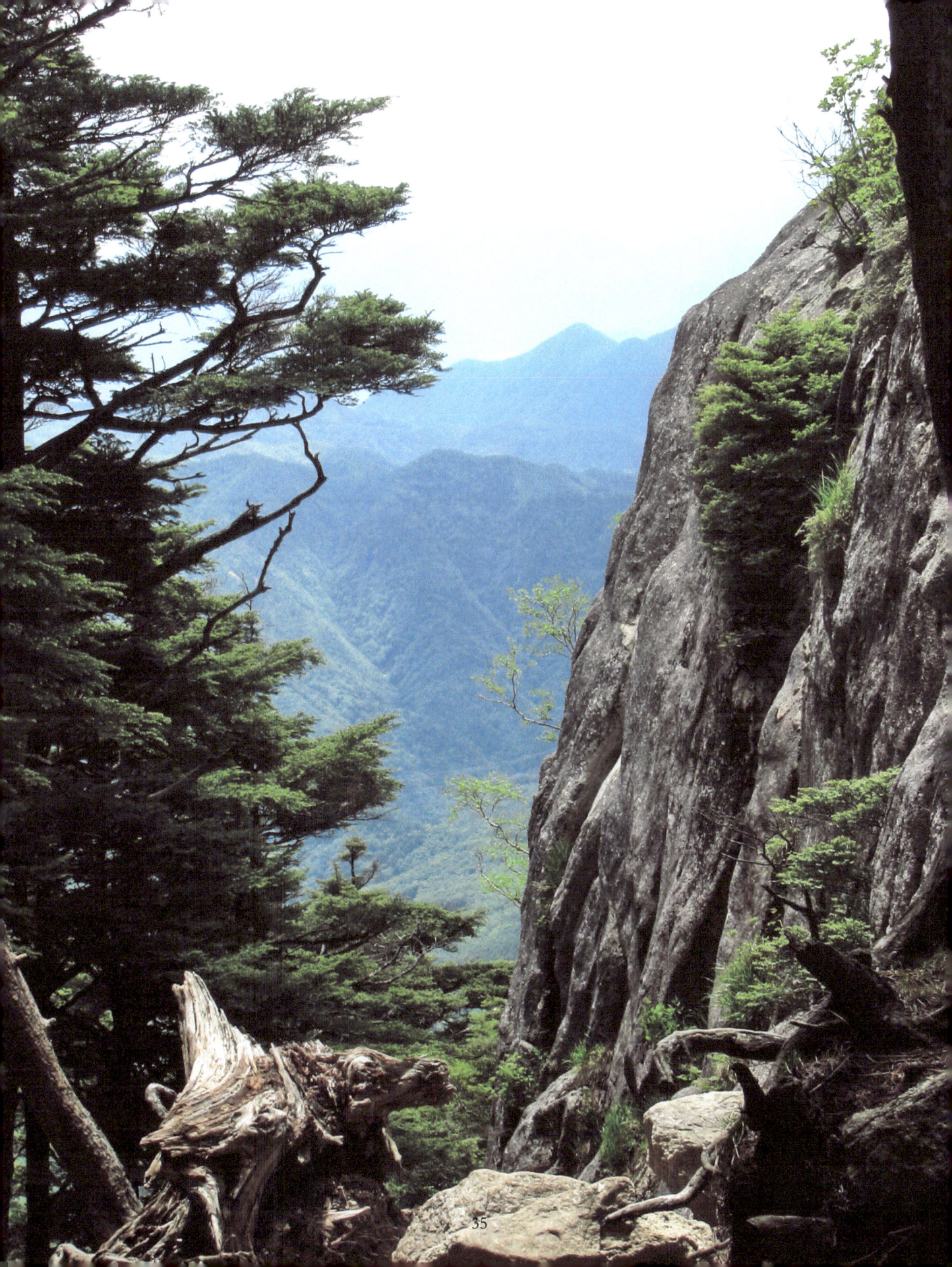

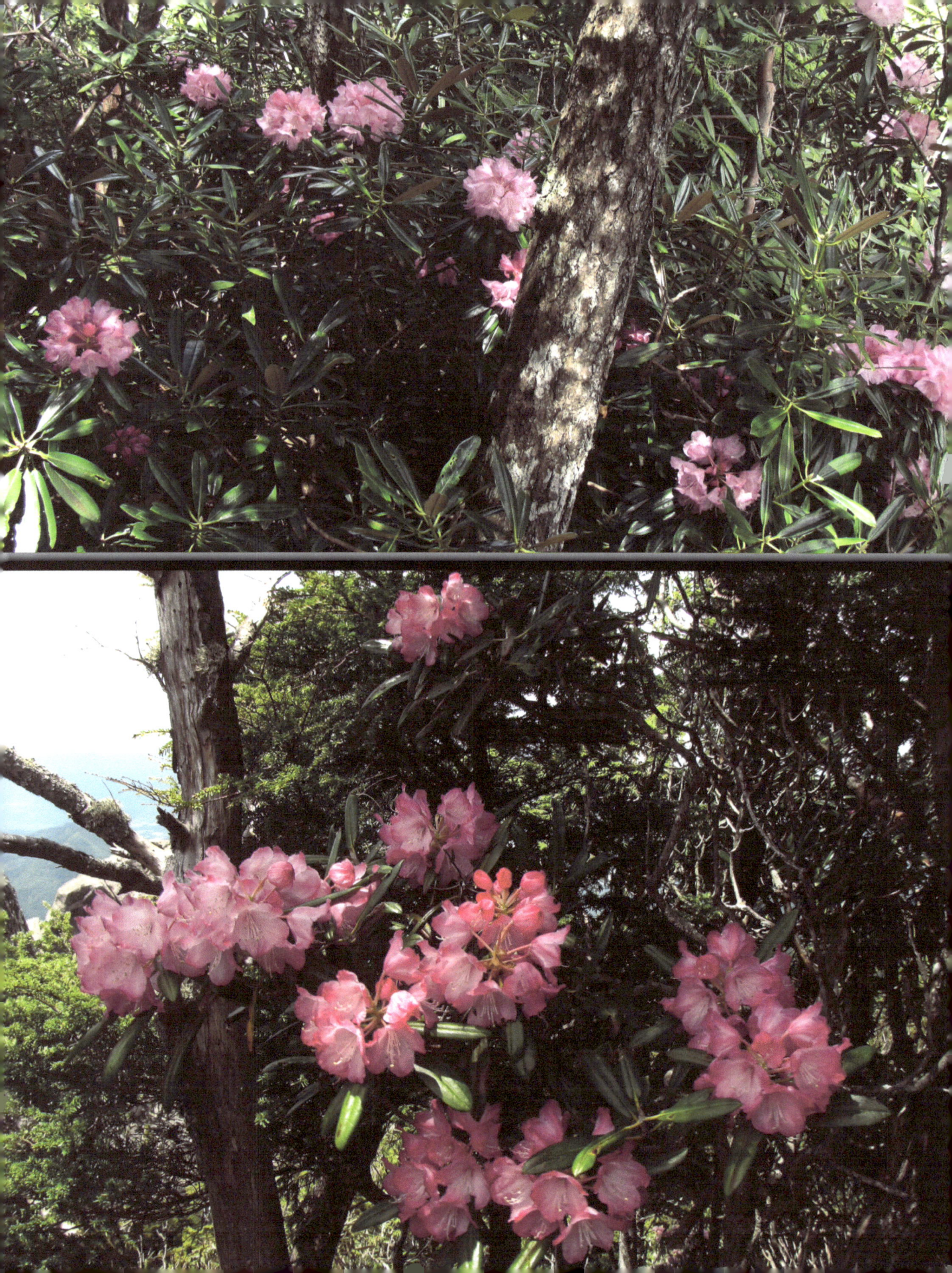

The photo on page 35 (2 pages back) shows a huge rock which we passed just below at 12:11 PM, just about 10 minutes below the summit. In this photo the trees which can be seen in the immediate area all look as if they are barely hanging on. On the left you can see a tree which is leaning over to the left quite severely and you can also see the roots of a tree which has fallen over on the left. On the right you can see the roots of that tree are jutting out of the soil and it appears that most of the soil on the lower side of that tree has washed away. We cannot specifically recall this precise location, but it is possible that this is happening due to this trail. So many people use these mountain trails here in Japan that many of them have turned into erosion gullies on the sides of the mountains. It is entirely possible that is what has happened here.

The photos on page 36 (the facing page) are the 2nd and final flowering species which you will find in this volume. This is of course rhododendron, and specifically it is *Rhododendron degronianum*. These were taken just below the summit. There were quite a number of these beautiful flowering rhododendrons in a small area. In some areas of various countries rhododendrons are a nuisance species which people curse quite loudly, but here in Japan – at least in the areas where we hang out – they are a relative rarity and are appreciated by flower lovers such as ourselves.

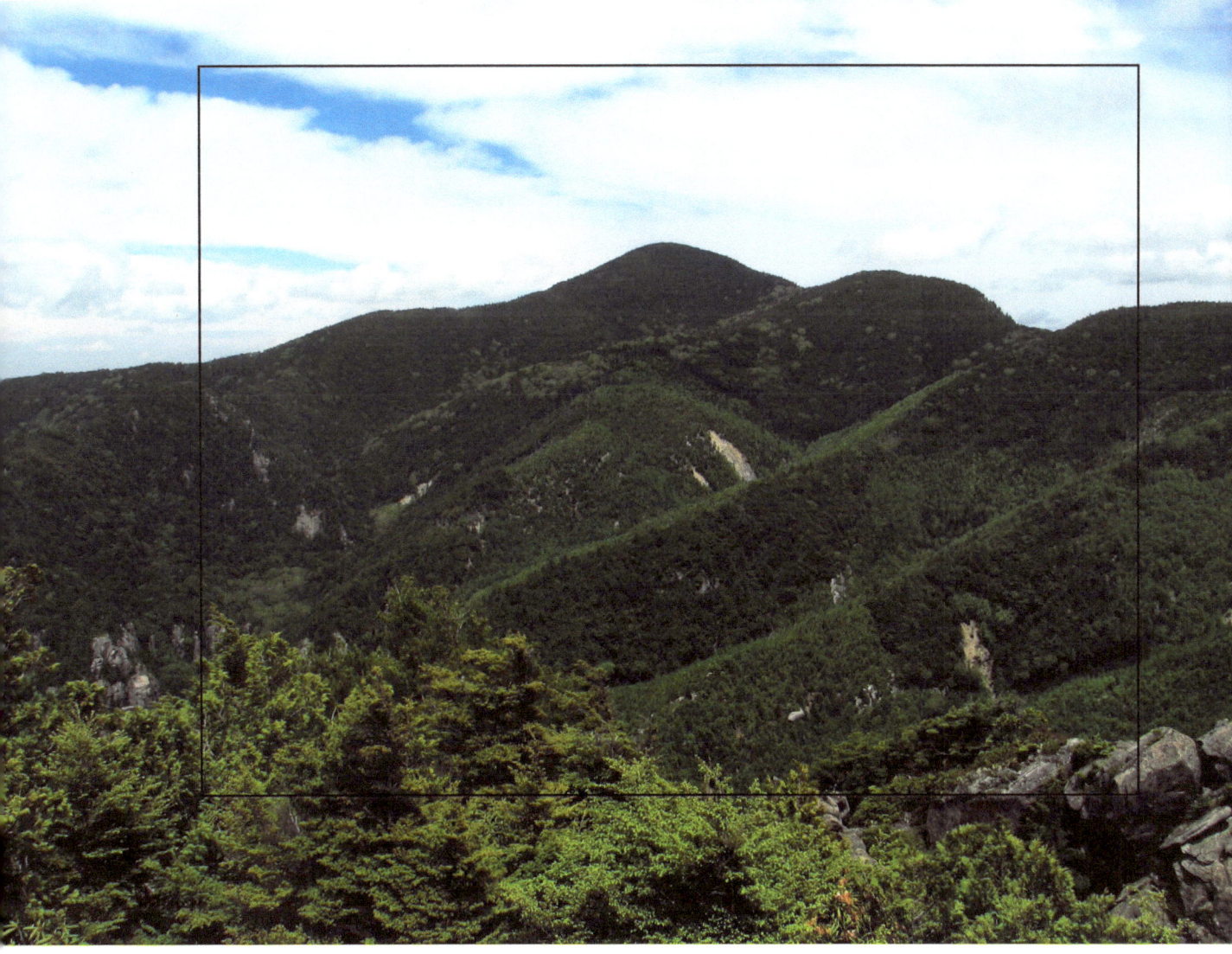

The photo on the previous page was taken from the summit of Mt. Mizugaki at 12:23 PM. We think that we remember that it was taken while looking approximately east-southeast. Mt. Kinpu would be to the right of this photo. We'll show you a photo or two of Mt. Kinpu later on. The outlined area in that previous photo shows the approximate area which is shown in the next photo, which was, of course, zoomed in. That haze which was so obvious previously seems to have mostly disappeared.

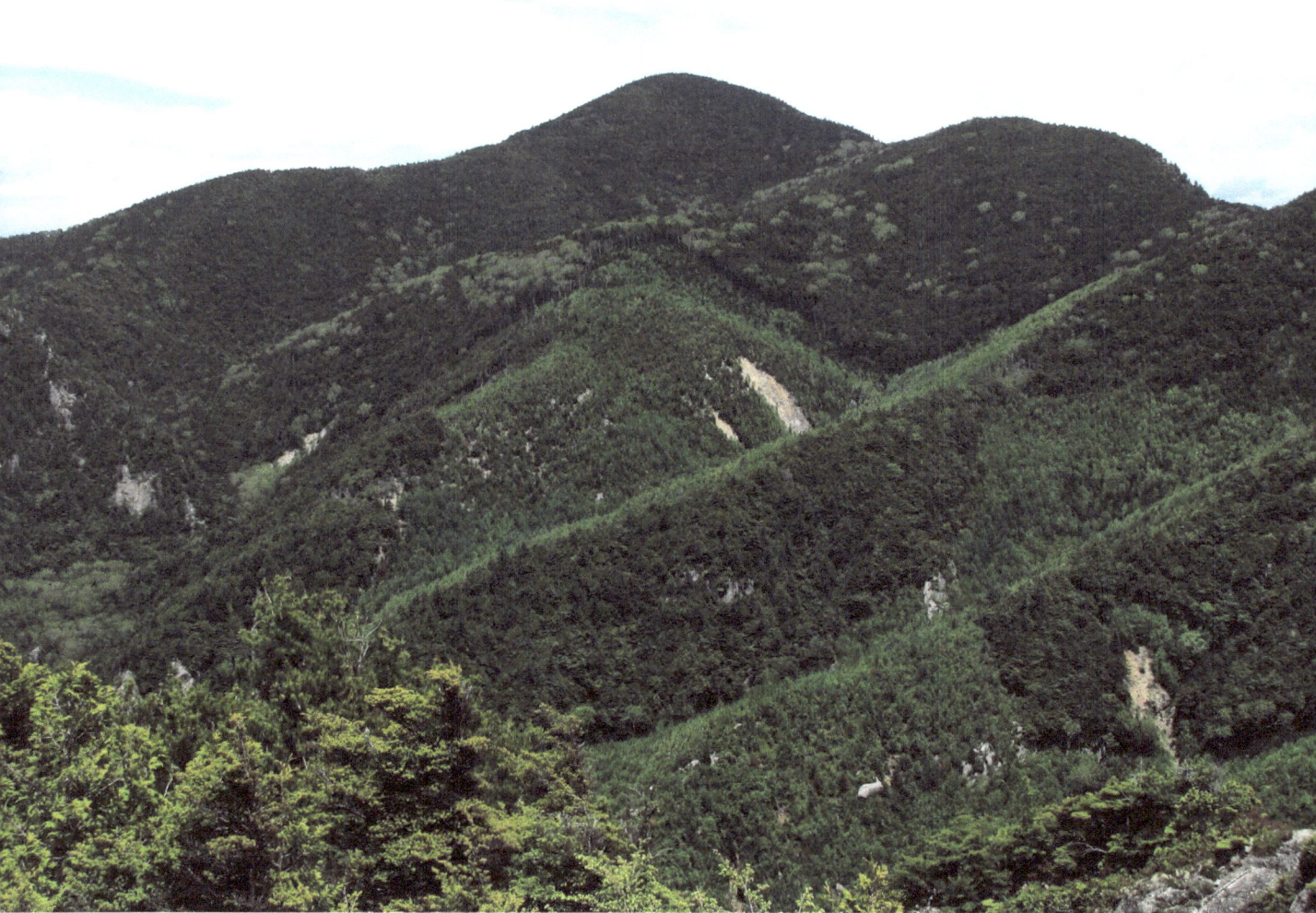

The upper photo on the facing page is a rocky scenery view which was taken while looking pretty much due east from the summit of Mt. Mizugaki and it was taken at 12:24 PM. Looking back, we should have taken more panoramic shots than we did. Oh well, maybe next time. There was no view from the summit looking in a northerly direction because there was a clump of trees to the north which effectively blocked the view.

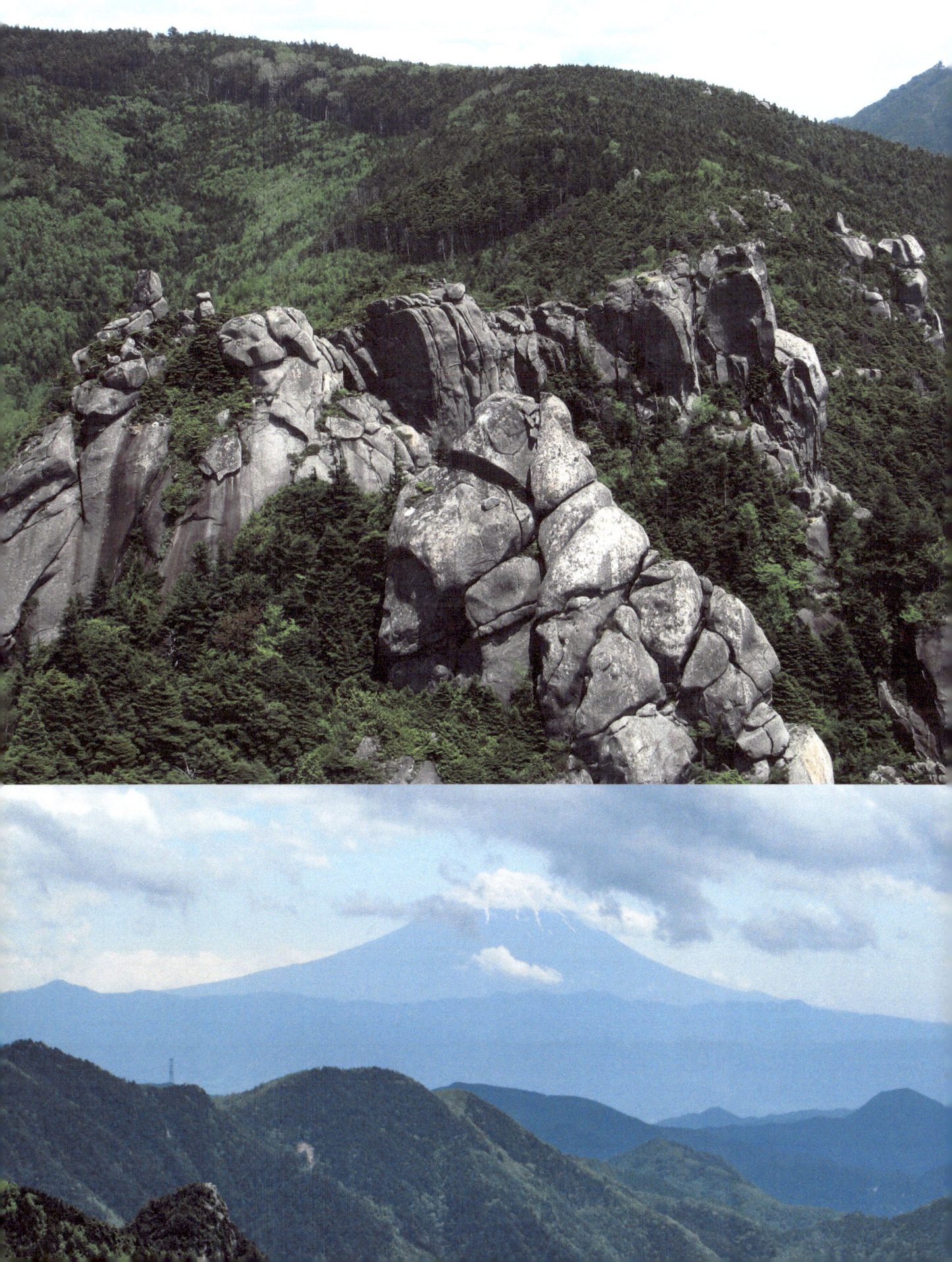

The lower photo on the previous page shows Mt. Fuji in the center of the photo – the mountain with its head in the clouds. Mt. Fuji is just a very few degrees east of due south from Mt. Mizugaki. This photo was shot at 12:26 PM.

The photo just below was taken at 12:27 PM and in this photo you can see Mt. Kinpu. It is a bit to the right of the center of the photo and the rocky summit sticks up prominently. If you go back to the map on page 9 you will notice that Mt. Kinpu is off the edge of the map to the southeast. It is not very far off the edge of the map, about 1 inch (= 2.5 cm) at the very most. In this photo, if you study it very diligently you can find a hut (outlined in black on this photo), which is most likely the Mt. Kinpu Hut. That hut is supposed to be about twenty minutes below the 2,598 m (= 8,524 ft) summit of Mt. Kinpu.

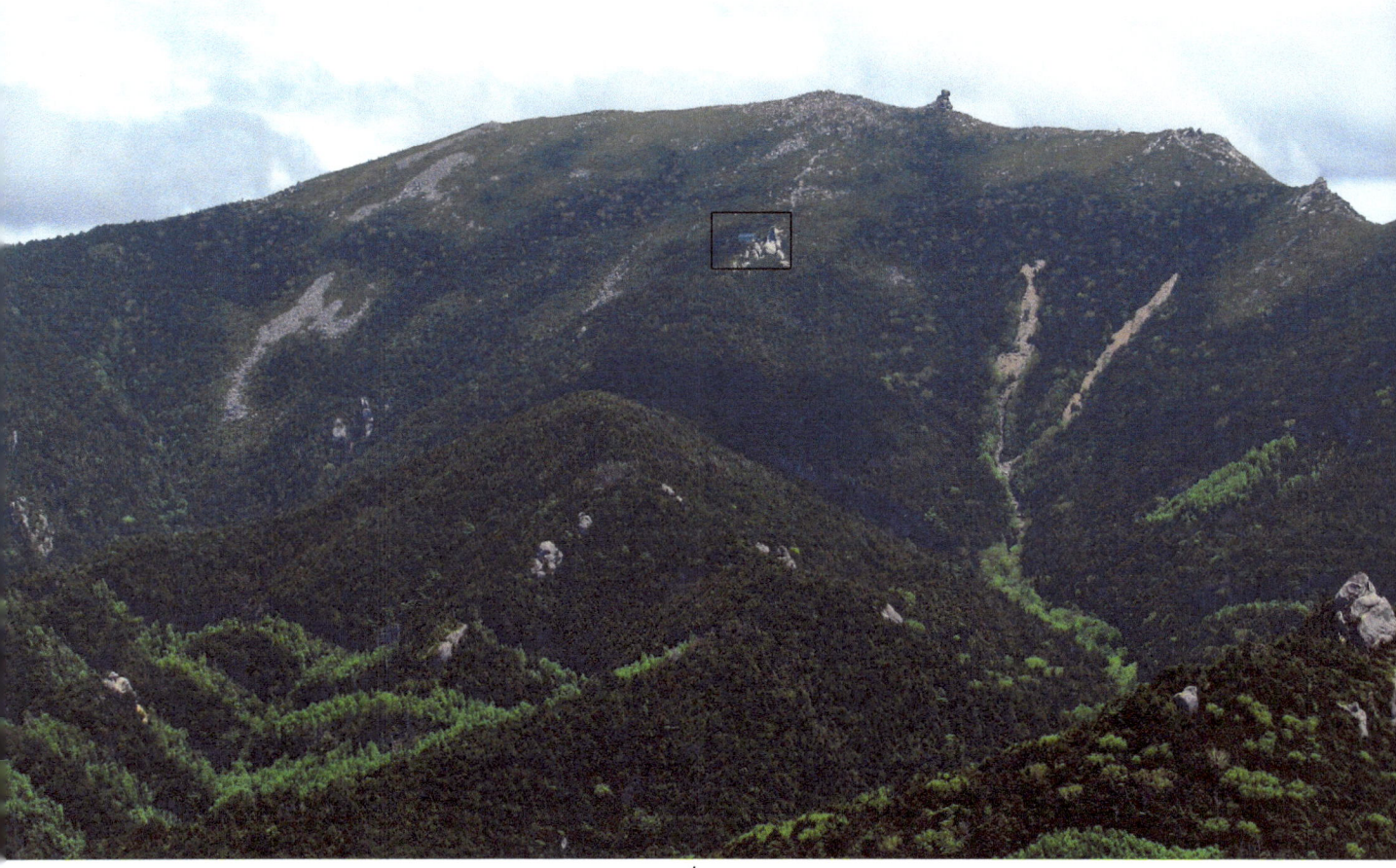

The facing page photo, a full page panoramic spread of two photos, shows the scenery from Mt. Fuji, on the right, to the lower slopes of the Mt. Kinpu ridgeline, on the left. It's a very nice view and you will surely notice that the haze which was prominent earlier, is now totally gone.

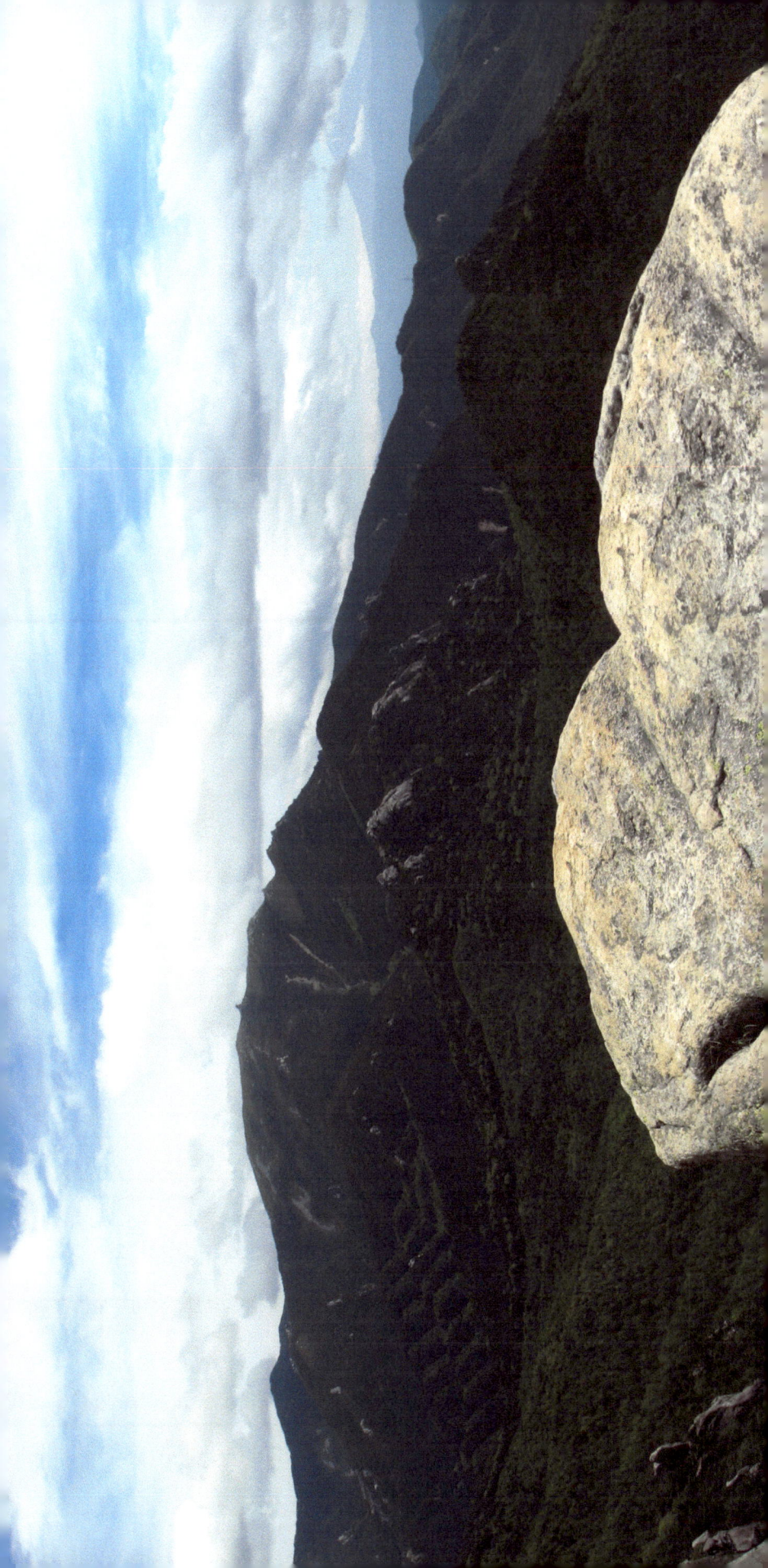

The photo just below is of me walking around on the summit of Mt. Mizugaki. It was taken at 12:29 PM. You can see the summit sign, written in Japanese kanji characters. The mountain with its head in the clouds which is on the right side of the photo, and also to the right of me is Mt. Yatsugatake. Too bad that it is clouded in at this time. You may have noticed, back on the list of 100 Famous Mountains, that we have summited Mt. Yatsugatake. Therefore we will be doing a volume on Mt. Yatsugatake. It seems that it will be Volume 13 in this series.

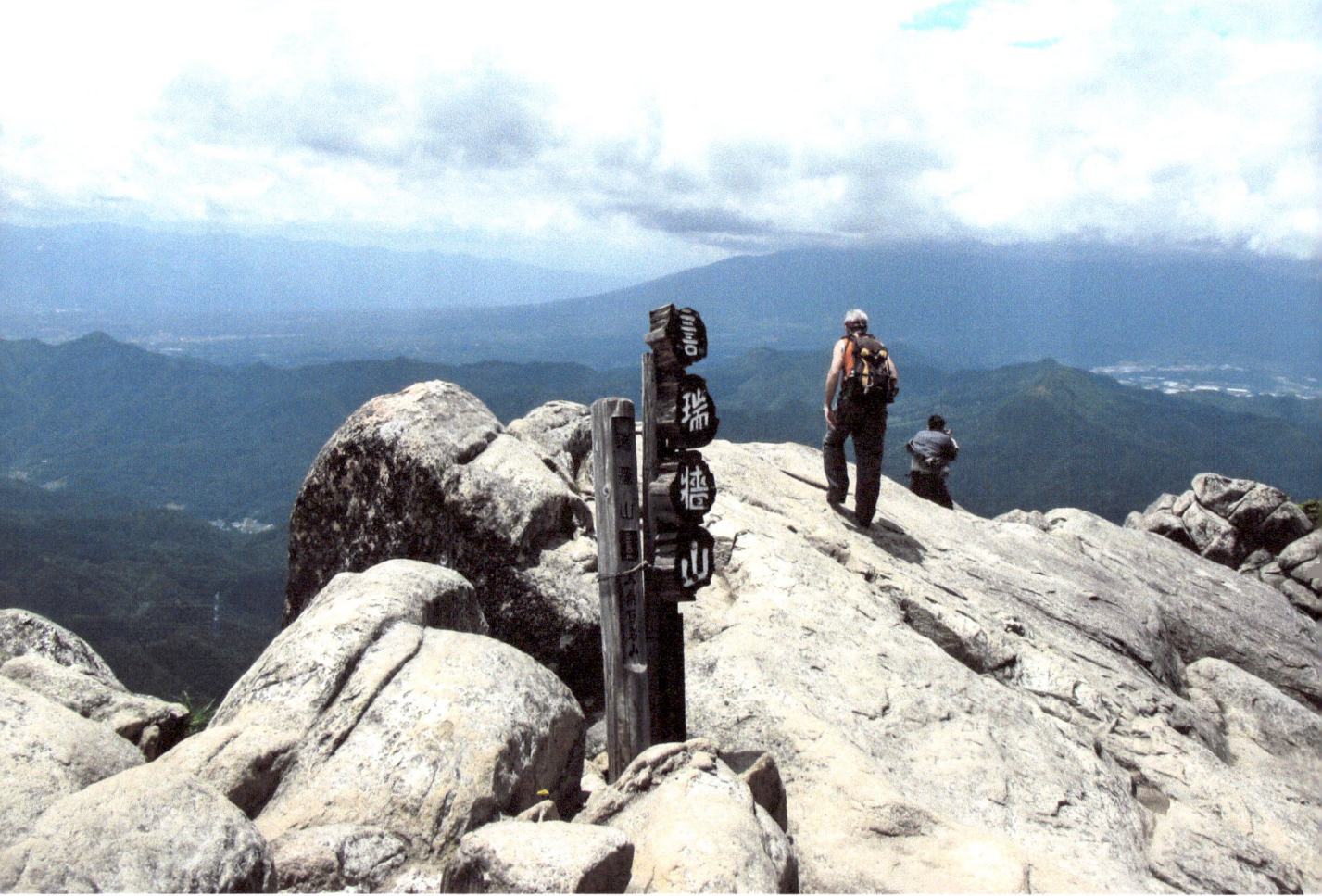

The shot on the facing page is another one of that rock pillar which we showed you a few times already, most recently back on page 34. In that photo we were just about level with the top of the pillar. You will surely notice that now we are well above the top of this pillar. If you study this photo closely you can once again see two climbers. You may also notice that the red colored windbreaker jacket which is visible in the inset photo on page 34 is still there.

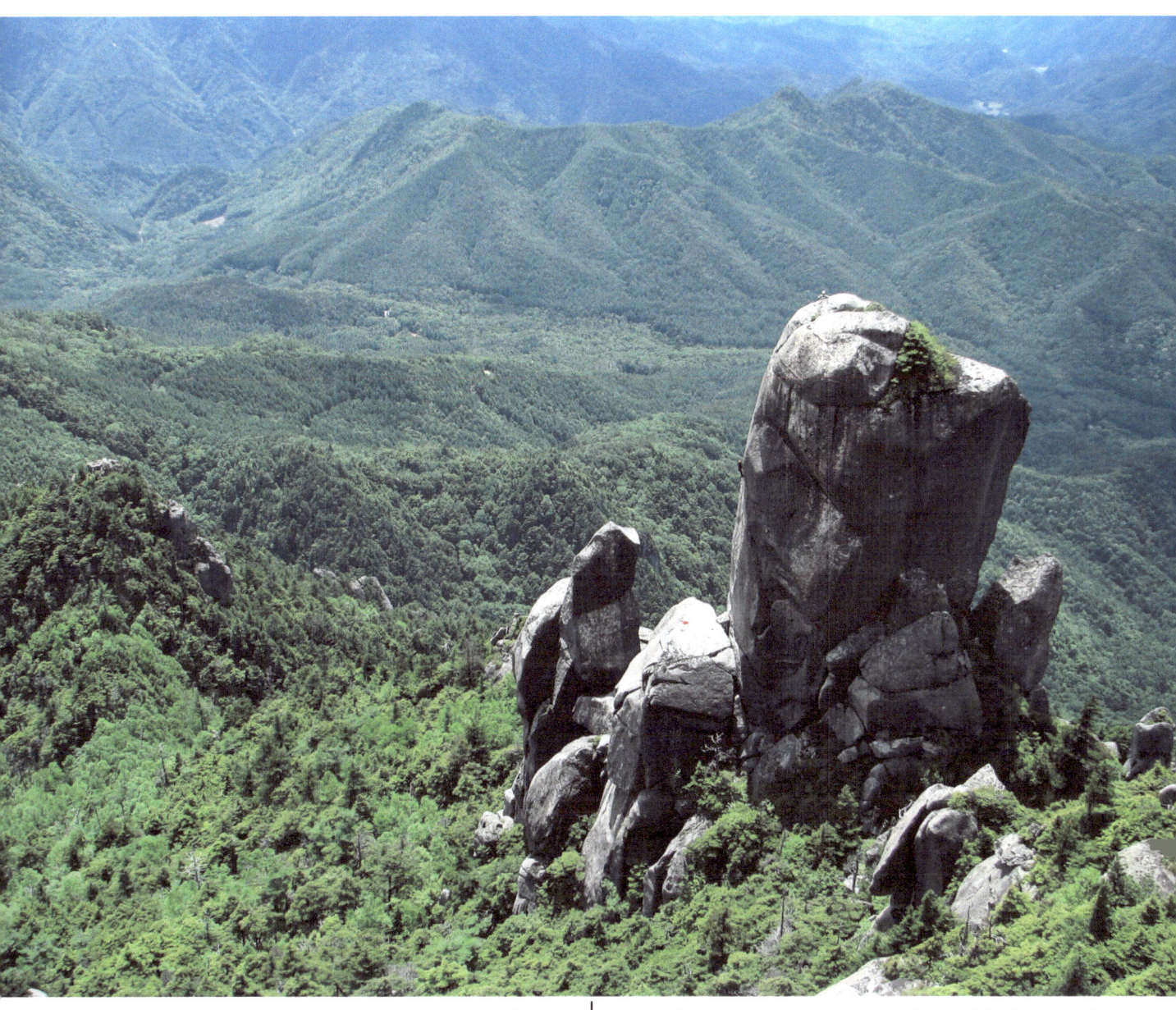

Now we're going to show you two photos which are quite similar, but different enough so that we wanted to show you both of them. They both show amazing rocky scenery. In the following photo you can see no people, to us that looks like the type of place that somebody should want to be on top of on this beautiful weather day. Is it too difficult, or is it not difficult enough to attract the technical climbers? The wind was blowing like a banshee here at this elevation at this time, was that why nobody was climbing on this rock?

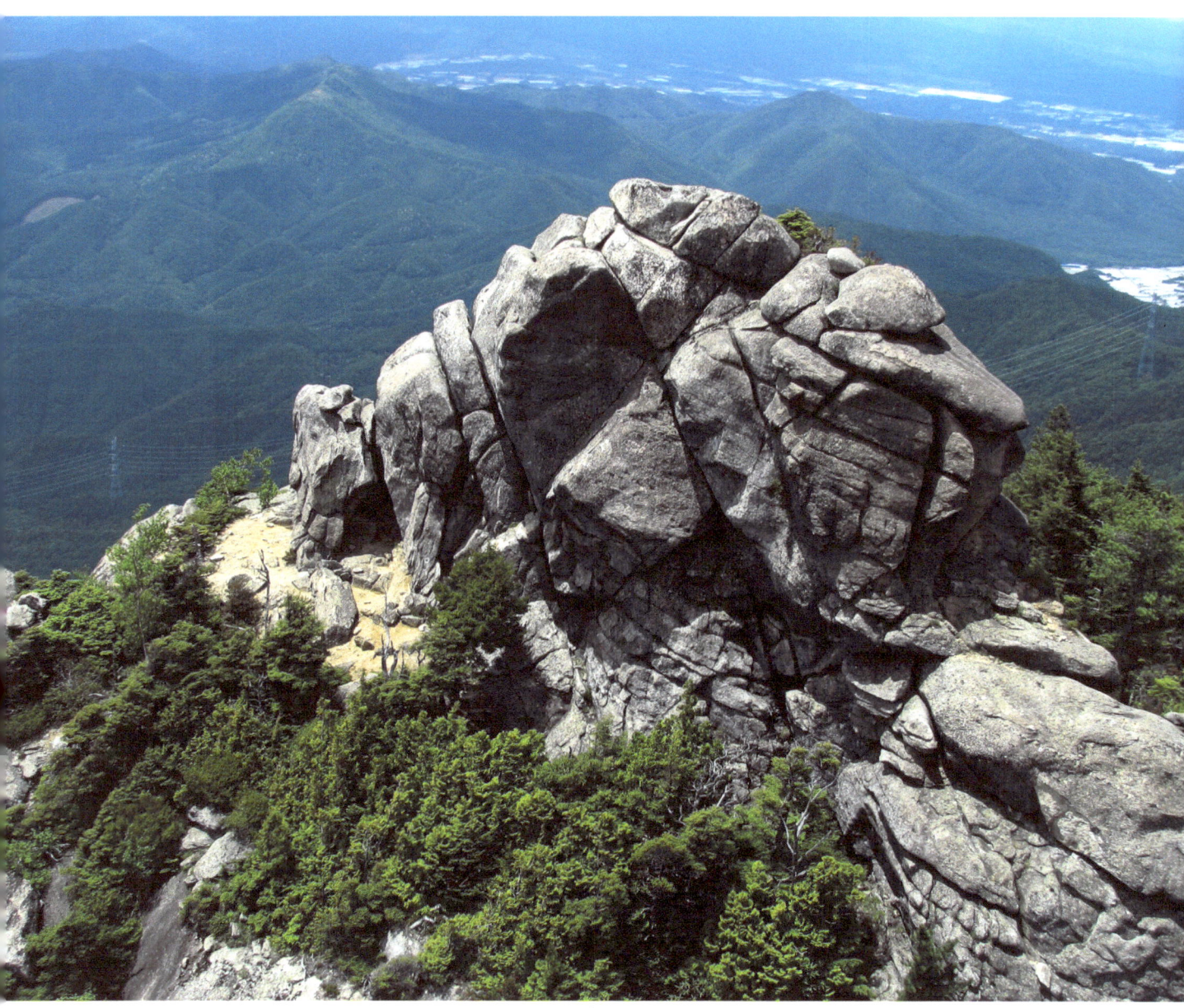

The second photo of this intriguing rock is on the facing page. In this photo you can see that it falls off vertically on the left side, but we cannot recall what the right side looks like and for some reason, none of our photos show what that right side looks like.

In this photo you can again see Mt. Yatsugatake off in the distance, with its head hiding in the clouds. Mt. Yatsugatake is about 22 km (13.6 miles) from here at a heading of very close to west-northwest. Anyway, this is such an intriguing rock!

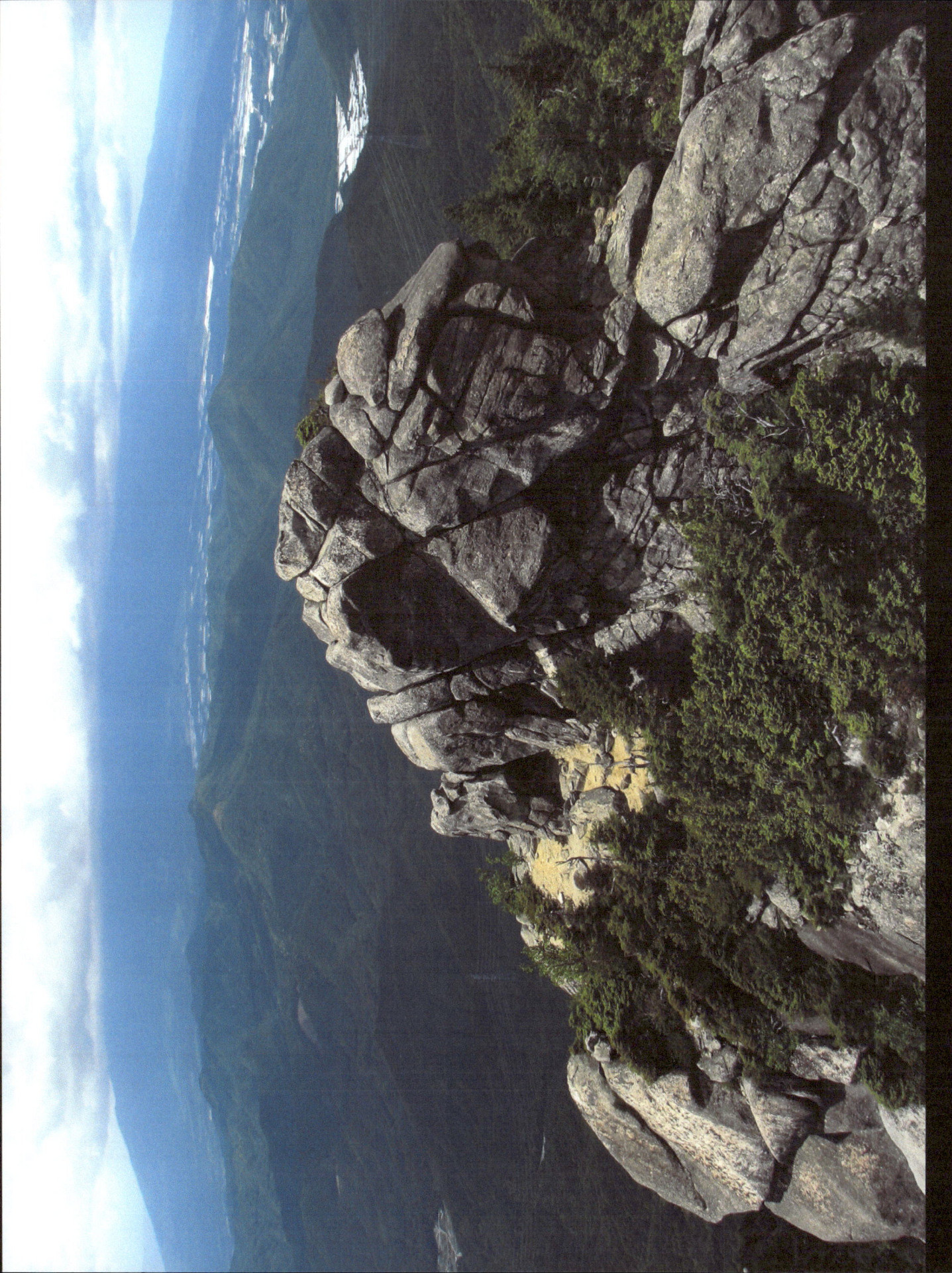

Just below is one of the summit markers – you saw another one back on page 42. You cannot see this spot in any of our photos. It is quite large, so it is placed a short distance below the summit on a flatter spot. You may notice that the mountain name – Mt. Mizugaki – is carved into this marker using hiragana characters. Do you recall back on page 7 when we stated that most of the signs in the area which direct one to this mountain are written in Hiragana (みずがき) because very few Japanese people can even read the kanji for Mizugaki (瑞牆山)? Here is a fine example of this.

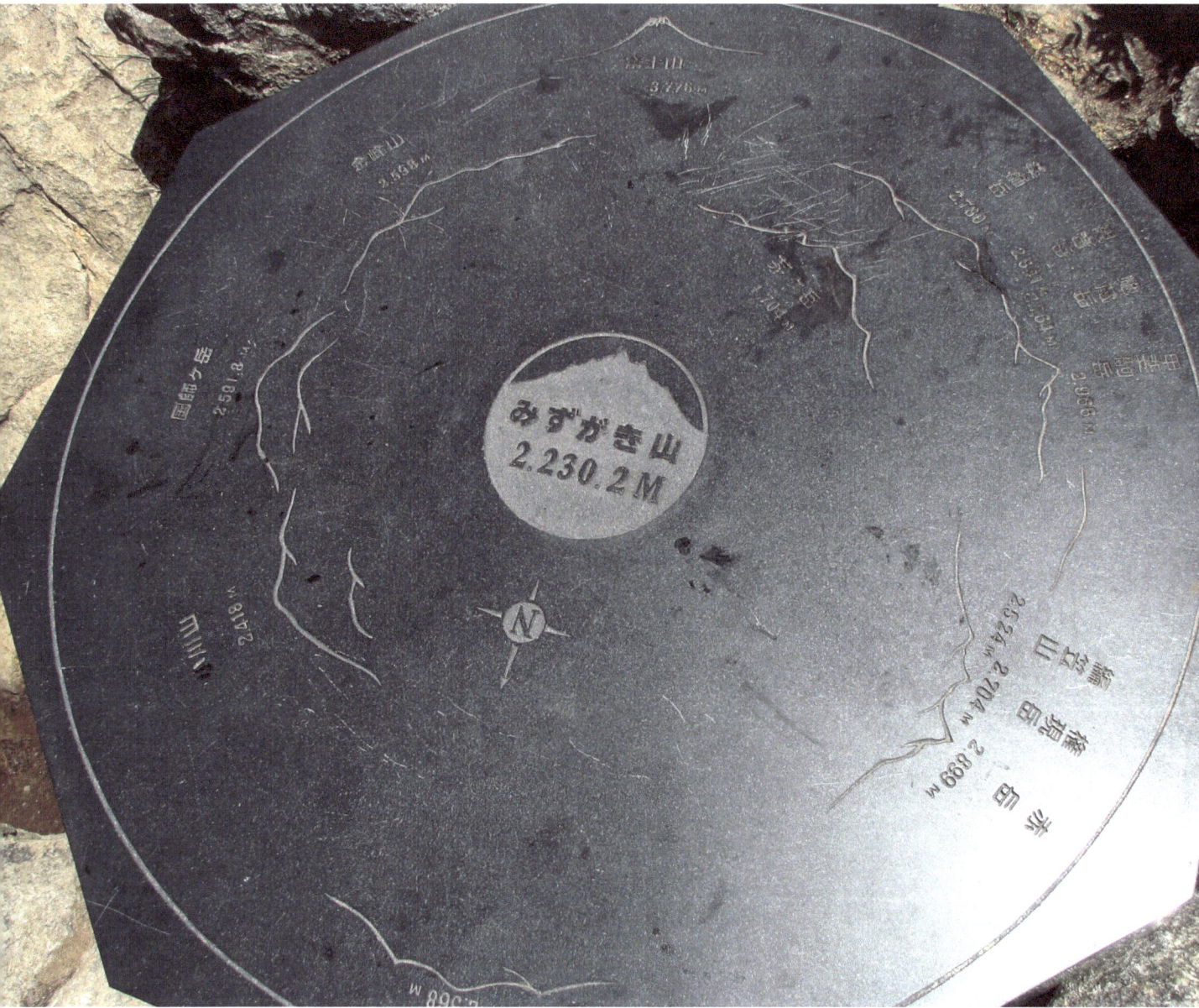

The facing page photo is quite similar to the upper photo back on page 39, but it shows more area to the right and that is the reason we are showing it to you. One day we'd like to return to this mountain and do more exploring in this general area.

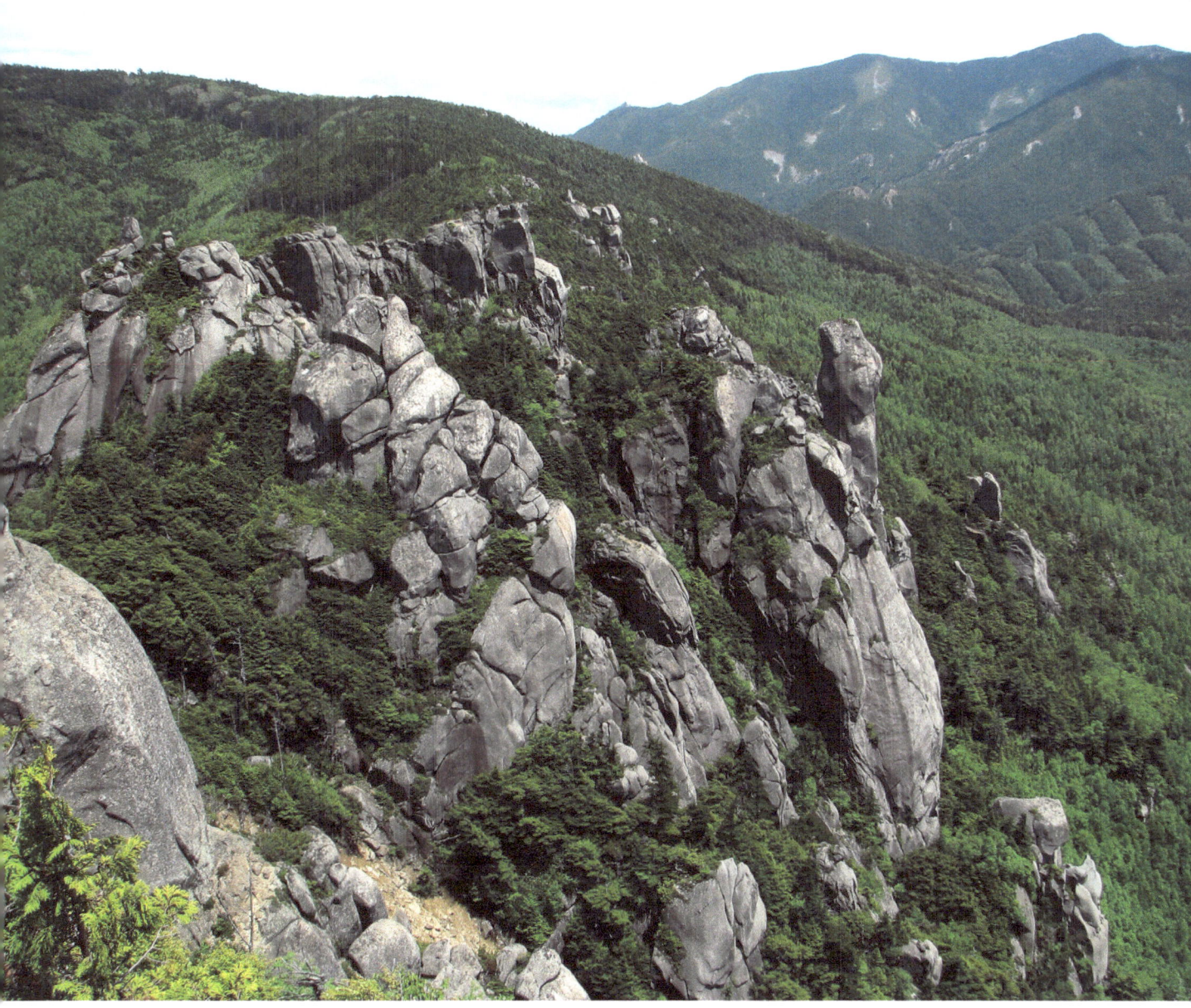

The next image shows two separate shots of each of us at the summit marker. On this marker the mountain name is written using Japanese kanji instead of hiragana characters. Please don't ask us why.

Back on page 43 we told you that the wind was blowing like a banshee at this elevation, and in this image that is fairly obvious from the way that our hair is blowing around and making us look rather like wild men. These two photos were taken at about 12:50 PM, just a short time before we headed back down to the bus stop. Note how happy and satisfied we appear when we are on mountains.

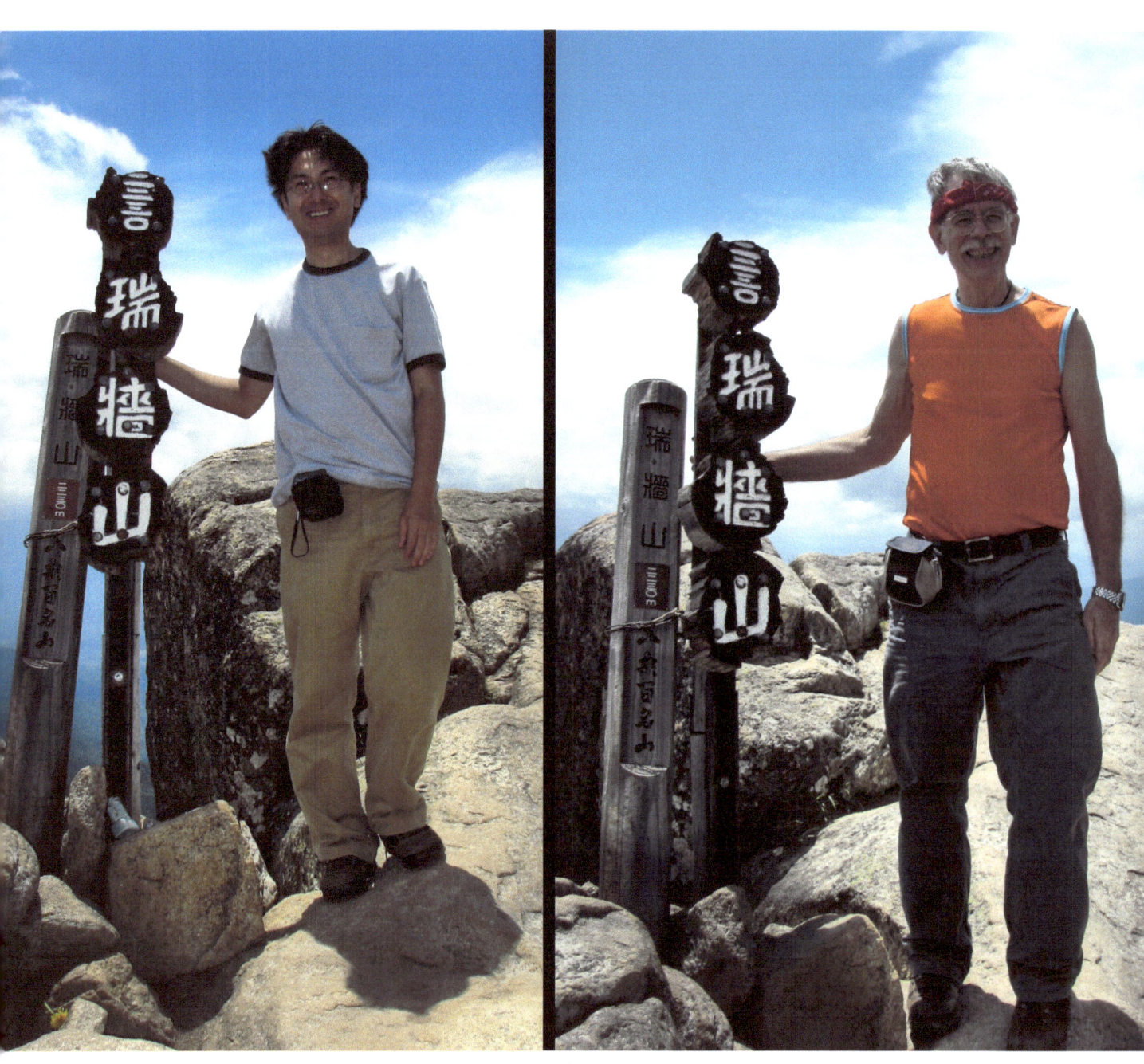

The facing page photo was taken 12:54 PM, just as we were starting back down. It was taken from right beside the round summit marker shown back on page 46. The person standing there most likely does not realize how nicely he is posing for the camera, with the beautiful blue sky behind him. He is probably standing like that to brace himself against the cool wind, but whatever the reason, thank you for your efforts!

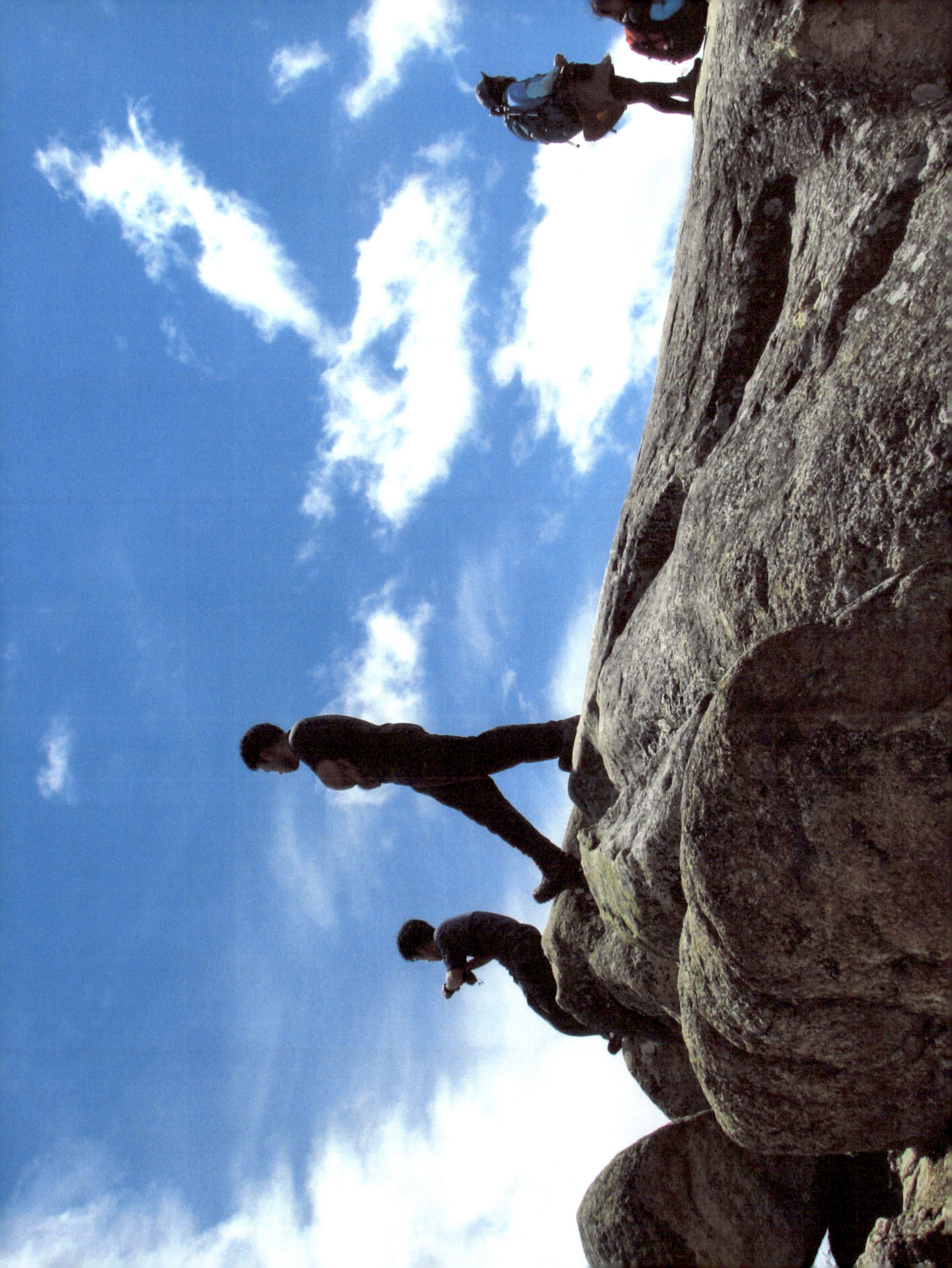

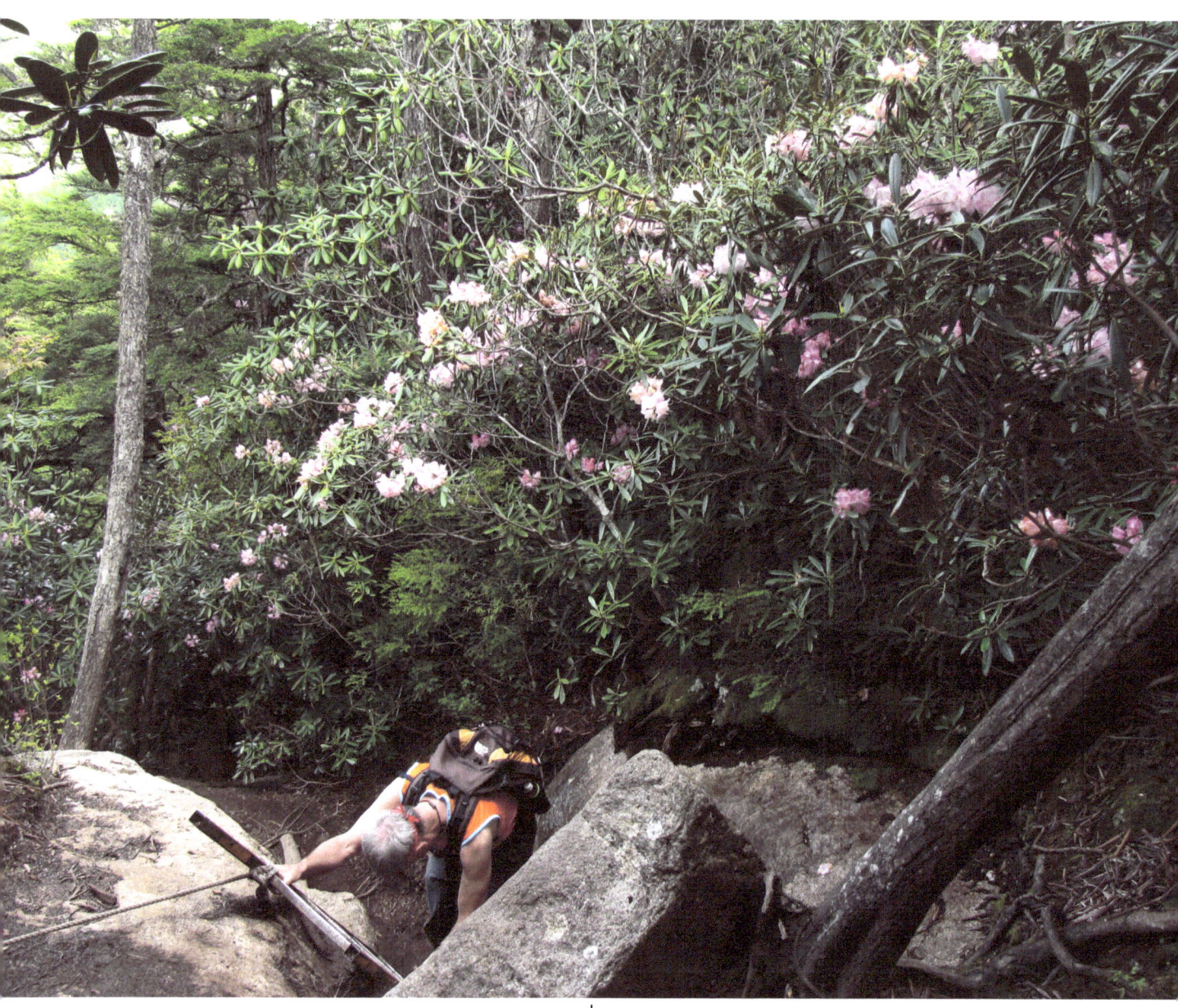

The photo just above shows me at 12:57 PM. If you look at the map back on page 9 you'll note how one comes to this mountain from the south, but then the final short distance is from the north. The reason for this is because it's vertical rock on the south face. Even as one approaches on the trail, the last little portion is ropes and ladders. This photo shows a rope leading to a ladder and I am descending the ladder at this time. Of course you will notice the rhododendron, (*Rhododendron degronianum*) in the background.

The facing page photo shows me descending via a rope at 12:59 PM. If we remember correctly, this is the final difficulty before being back on normal trail.

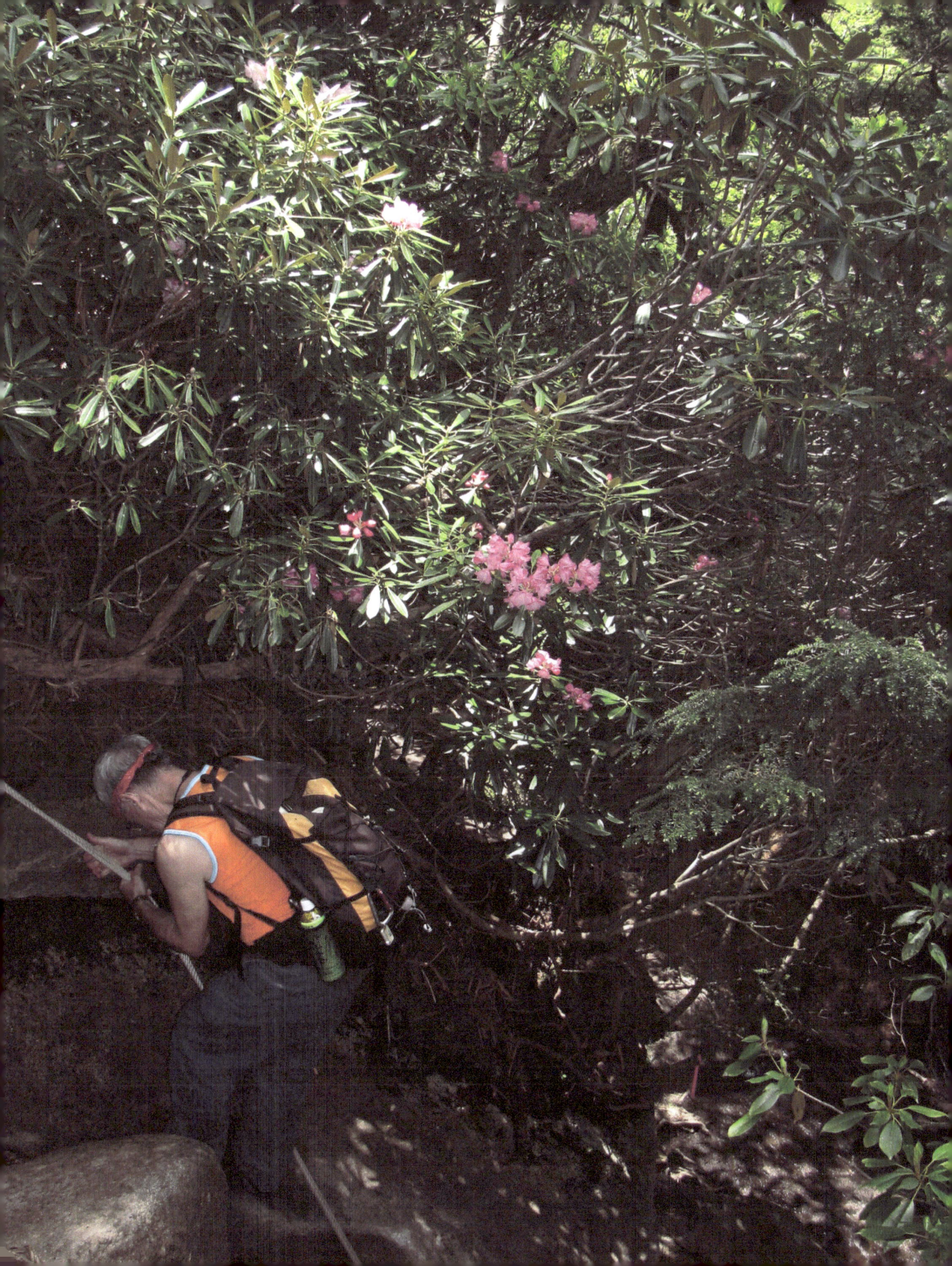

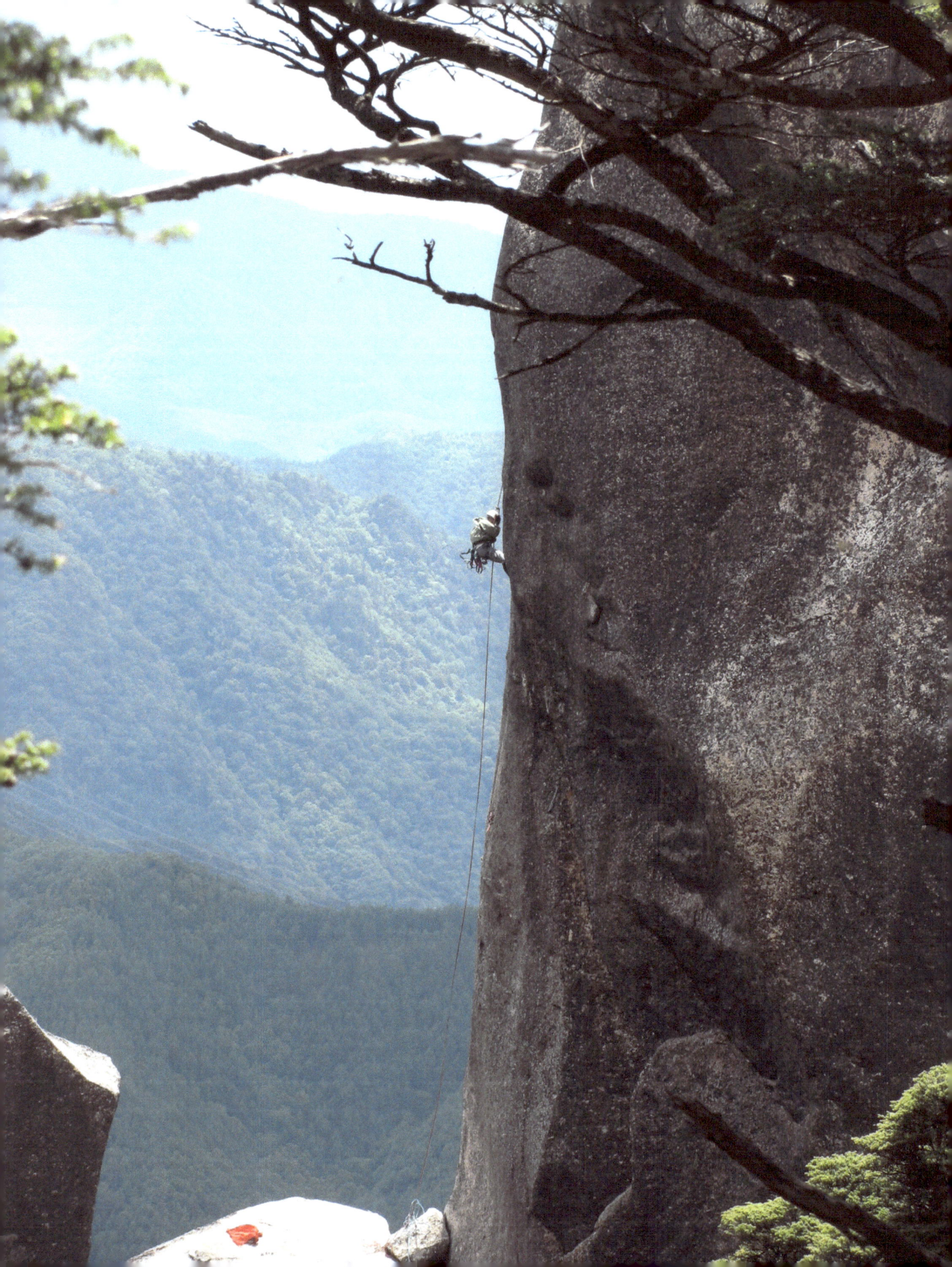

As we passed closest to that rock pillar, which we have shown you several photos of before this, there was a climber rappelling down it. You'll note that the red windbreaker, or whatever it is, is still lying on the rock. It seems like it should have blown away by now, so maybe it's not a windbreaker at all, maybe it's a gear bag and still has some considerable weight of climbing gear in it. Who knows, not us, that's for certain.

Here is the final photo from this climb of Mt. Mizugaki – with its very complex kanji (瑞牆山). Such a beautiful blue sky with some nice puffy cumulus clouds moving around. Such a nice way to send us on our way down the mountain.

We sincerely hope that you are enjoying this series of books. If you would like any further information about any of these mountains there is a great abundance of it available on the internet. If you want to e-mail me with specific questions you may do so through the link on my website, which is http://danwiz.com. I hope to maintain this site as long as I am alive.

THE END

ABOUT THE AUTHORS

Daniel Wieczorek was born in 1947 in Ionia, Michigan. He graduated from the University of Michigan with a B.S. in Forestry in 1969. He moved to Oregon to work in the field of forestry in 1971. That was followed by a move to Alaska in 1975, where he continued his career in forestry. After about a 14 year career in forestry, Daniel decided to do something different and he served as a Peace Corps Volunteer in The Philippines from 1985 – 1987. Upon completion of his Peace Corps service he returned to Alaska, where he attended the University of Alaska – Fairbanks and received an M.B.A. in 1991. This was followed by a move to South Korea in 1992, where Daniel taught English to Korean people wishing to improve their English Language skills. Daniel's next stop was in New York City, where he worked as temporary staff at Deutsche Bank from 1998 – 2001. He left NYC in March 2001 and moved on to his present home in Mitaka City, Tokyo, Japan. He is teaching English in Japan and at this time he's been teaching as a career for about 17 years. He has been hiking, climbing and doing photography since he was about 12 years old.

Kazuya Numazawa was born in 1979 in Shinjo in Yamagata Prefecture, Japan. He was raised in Funagata Town in Yamagata Prefecture. He graduated from Tokyo University in 2005. Since that time he has worked in several fields, but primarily in Cram Schools around the Mitaka Area.

Daniel and Kazuya met in 2001 and they have been hiking, mountain climbing and doing photography together since that time and generally enjoying life together.

NOTES

Photo Credits:

Daniel's Photos:

Pages 7, 8, 9, 11, 12, 13 top, 14 all, 15, 16, 17, 19, 20, 24, 25, 26, 27, 28, 29, 30, 32, 33 all, 35, 37, 38, 39 all, 40, 43, 44, 45, 46, 47, 48 left, 49, 53.

Kazuya's Photos:

Pages 10, 13 bottom, 18 all, 21, 22, 23, 31, 34 all, 36 all, 41, 42, 48 right, 50, 51, 52.

www.ingramcontent.com/pod-product-compliance
Lightning Source LLC
Chambersburg PA
CBHW050745180526
45159CB00003B/1353